Missouri Woman's Missionary Union's

Centennial Journey

1923-2023

Jeannie,

Thanks for your interest in Missouri missions!

Jan Turner
MWMU President
4/16/2023

Copyright © 2023 Jan Turner

Under International Copyright Law, no part of this publication may be reproduced, stored, or transmitted by any means–electronic, mechanical, photographic (photocopy), recording, or otherwise–without written permission from Missouri Woman's Missionary Union.

Missouri Woman's Missionary Union is an auxiliary to the Missouri Baptist Convention.

ISBN: 9798375117287

Printed in the United States of America
Cover Design by Sarah Turner
Cover Photo taken in Osage Beach, MO by Kenny Eliason
[Unsplash.com]
Interior Design by C. A. Simonson
First Printing 2023

Missouri Woman's Missionary Union's

Centennial Journey

1923-2023

Compiled and Written by

Jan Turner

Dedication

To those Missouri WMU Women who have served the last 100 years as WMU Executive Directors, WMU Presidents, WMU Board Members, WMU staff, and church WMU leaders by dedicating their time and service to increase missions' awareness in Missouri. These women are examples of the permanent WMU watchword, "For we are laborers together with God." I Corinthians 3:9a (Modern English Version)

Contents

Dedication v

Acknowledgments viii

Foreword xi

Preface xiii

Chapter 1 - The Beginning 15

Chapter 2 - The Leadership of Mable Lyne Reynolds 20

Chapter 3 - The Presidency of Laura Malotte Armstrong 23

Chapter 4 - The Presidency of Cora Cowgill McWilliams 30

Chapter 5 - The Leadership of Madge Nicholson Truex 32

Chapter 6 - The Presidency of Louise Enloe McKee 35

Chapter 7 - The Presidency of Josephine Riley Medlin 38

Chapter 8 - The Presidency of LeeAnna Floy Kinell 40

Chapter 9 - The Leadership of Eva Berry 42

Chapter 10 - The Presidency of Lena Shaner Burnham 48

Chapter 11 - The Leadership of Hilda Beggs 51

Chapter 12 - The Presidency of Elizabeth Tillery Crozier 55

Chapter 13 - The Leadership of Mary O. Bidstrup 60

Chapter 14 - The Presidency of Eunice Powell Allison 64

Chapter 15 - The Presidency of Ferroll Woodford Delozier ...69

Chapter 16 - The Presidency of Viola Volkart Scherff 77

Chapter 17 - The Leadership of Alberta Gilpin 83

Chapter 18 - The Presidency of Marilyn Harris Coble 104

Chapter 19 - The Presidency of Lorene Hamblen Murphy 109

Chapter 20 - The Presidency of Barbara Birt Bray 117

Chapter 21 - The Presidency of Norma Hays Altis 129

Chapter 22 - The Presidency of Dawn O'Neill Phillips 140

Chapter 23 - The Presidency of Barbara Daniels Popp 153

Chapter 24 - The Presidency of Debbie Bailey Miller 166

Chapter 25 - The Leadership of Kathy Stahr Scott......................176

Chapter 26 - The Leadership of Vivian Hargrove McCaughan...179

Chapter 27 - The Presidency of Lorraine Rogers Powers............187

Chapter 28 - The Presidency of Joan Harms Dotson...................196

Chapter 29 - The Leadership of Laura Adams Wells 209

Chapter 30 - The Presidency of Cherri Hall Crump 211

Chapter 31 - The Leadership of Bonnie Hildreth Carter 219

Chapter 32 - The Presidency of Mary Ann Collier Randall 223

Chapter 33 - The Presidency of Connie Meeker Craig................225

Chapter 34 - The Presidency of Jan Currence Turner..................228

Chapter 35 - The Leadership of Cheryl Marler Stahlman 243

Chapter 36 - Lesotho-Missouri Prayer Partnership 246

Epilogue 260

Appendix I 265

MISSOURI WMU ANNUAL MEETING LOCATIONS 265

Appendix II 269

MISSOURI WMU PRESIDENTS 1923-2023............................ 269

Appendix III..271

MISSOURI WMU EXECUTIVE DIRECTORS 1923-2023 271

Appendix IV..272

MISSOURI EMERITUS MISSIONARIES 2006-2023.............. 272

Appendix V 273

MISSOURI WMU NOTEWORTHY EVENTS 1923-2023 273

Chapter Notes..282

Bibliography 290

About The Author..291

vii

Acknowledgments

If you will note on the title page, I'm listed as both the compiler and the writer. Of the two, I think I'm more of a compiler because much of this book is taken from previously published books, past MWMU Mission Celebration programs, MWMU Minutes, and MWMU Resource books. These written documents enabled me to put together 100 years of Missouri Woman's Missionary Union history, and I have tried to give them credit throughout the book. Some authors gave me permission to quote verbatim. To these authors, I am grateful.

I want to thank Laura Mason for giving me permission to use material from her two books, *Ye Are the Branches*, A History of Missouri Baptist Woman's Missionary Organizations, the history until 1986, and *Abide in Me*, a continuation of the history from 1987-1998. *Ye Are the Branches* was released in recognition of the 1988 centennial celebration of national WMU. *Abide in Me* was published as part of the 75th anniversary celebration of Missouri WMU in 1998.

Special thanks to Barbara Bray's daughter, Becky Moyer, who had saved her mother's manuscript and sent me a copy of *From Change to Challenge,* A Continuation of the History of the Missouri Woman's

Missionary Union from 1998-2007.

Thanks to Alberta Gilpin, who gave permission to use material from the book *Enduring Love, The Alberta Gilpin Story*, written by Barbara Bray.

I'm grateful for Randy Sprinkle and New Hope Publishing, Birmingham, for giving me permission to use portions of his book *"Until the Stars Appear."* Also, thanks to Randy Sprinkle and Teresa Flora for updating the Lesotho story.

I am grateful to the many people who were involved in the production of this book.

Thanks to former Communication Consultant on MWMU Board, Tammie Nichols, who summarized events from the 2008-2022 minutes.

Many of the former WMU historical documents and records were stored at the Partee Center at William Jewell College in Liberty, Missouri. I appreciate the help of Rebecca Hamlett, Librarian, in retrieving these documents. Thanks to Vivian Howell from Liberty for transporting the many historical document boxes to Jefferson City.

Thanks to Cindy Goodwin, volunteer Archivist at national WMU in Birmingham, and Julie Walters, Corporate Communications, for their assistance.

Carla Stegeman and Samantha Spencer from Missouri Baptist Convention staff were helpful in retrieving past WMU reports from the annual MBC Book of Reports.

Special thanks to the past MWMU Presidents and Executive Directors in recent years for writing their own story to include in this book. I appreciate the encouragement from Bonnie Carter, former MWMU Executive Director, who believed I could write this book.

I appreciate Angelia Carpenter, current MWMU Communications Consultant, for proofreading the manuscripts and researching publishing companies. I am grateful for Carol Bowers, current Prayer Advocate, for proofreading the manuscript. Brenda Poinsett, a Missouri WMU member, published author and friend of mine, graciously read the manuscript as it was in progress. She made punctuation, grammar, and spelling corrections. Brenda was a very detailed editor and made this book more readable and easier to understand. I am thankful for Brenda's expertise and encouragement.

Special thanks to Sarah Turner for the book cover design. I appreciate the work of Rev. Tommy Schmitt on the original cover design.

I appreciated so much C.A. Simonson, Publication Assistant, who assisted in getting the history formatted and ready for publication. Her expertise and experience as an author were invaluable.

Foreword

"So many wonderful, godly women have served in Missouri WMU over the past 100 years. Jan Turner has captured their hearts of giving, going, and spreading the gospel in Missouri and around the world. Don't miss learning about their legacy!"
-Laura Wells, Former Missouri WMU Executive Director, 2010-2019

"I enjoyed reading the *Centennial Journey* to be reminded about the people who were passionate about missions. It's a book about the ordinary women that God used, in extraordinary ways, to spread His story of love and grace to Missourians. Readers will hopefully be inspired to continue this legacy for another 100 years."
-Angelia Carpenter, MWMU Communications Consultant, Author, Conference Leader

"Having been a part of mission organizations in Missouri for almost three-fourths of the 100-year history of Missouri Woman's Missionary Union, I was intrigued by the many things I was not aware of regarding the legacy of the many faithful servants who held high the banner of missions by praying, giving, and going. Whether you are familiar with Missouri WMU or not, I believe you will be inspired as you read *Centennial Journey* and will desire to carry on this legacy into the next century by raising up a new generation to love missionaries, to pray, to give, and, most importantly, to go!"
-Carol Bowers, MWMU Prayer Advocate and International Mission Board Emeritus Missionary

xii

Preface

When I realized Missouri Woman's Missionary Union (MWMU) would be celebrating its 100th Anniversary in 2023, I thought it would be appropriate if an updated version of the history could be available for the celebration. I asked previously published authors if they would be interested in compiling and writing the MWMU's history. After being turned down three times, a couple of my friends said, "Jan, why don't you write it?" I thought about it and sensed that maybe I could do it. For the last fifty years, I have personally known the MWMU Presidents. A MWMU lady told me, "Jan, you have been in WMU forever." So, maybe that makes me a historical person!

The objective of the Woman's Missionary Union in 1923 was *"to promote Christian missions through the organization of Woman's Missionary Union in the churches of the Missouri Baptist Convention."* Today's mission statement for Missouri Woman's Missionary Union is *"Empowered by God's love, Missouri Woman's Missionary Union encourages and equips each individual and church to live a missional lifestyle."*

I hope you will gain a new appreciation for women of the past and present who have paved the way for missions to continue to make a difference in the lives of others.

Jan Turner

Missouri WMU President
January 2023

xiii

xiv

CHAPTER 1

The Beginning

When does the history of an organization begin? We usually associate an organization's birth with a particular date which we will do in this book as we trace the centennial missions' journey of Missouri Woman's Missionary Union. As an organization, they officially began October 15, 1923. But could the beginning have been before that? Perhaps in the movements that were taking place?

The reason I suggest this is because of the effect of some little objects called mite boxes. They were small boxes used to collect offerings—kind of a precursor to offering envelopes. These boxes were the idea of a Baltimore Methodist turned Baptist named Ann Jane Graves. In 1871, she organized Baptist women in her area to support women missionaries because the Foreign Mission Board was having difficulties providing support. She looked for ways to increase giving on a regular basis. She thought small boxes that could be inexpensively manufactured might be helpful.

Graves had paper boxes manufactured at a cost of four to six cents each. On one side was the name Woman's Gospel Mission to Women in Foreign

CHAPTER 1

Lands. A scripture verse printed on another side said, *To give light to them that sit in darkness* (Luke 1:79a). She encouraged women "to place in the box a definite amount—at least two cents—on a weekly basis." [1] She asked the women to regularly take their mite box offerings to church.

To those of us in the 21st century, that may sound simple and easy to do, but this was happening at a time of economic hardship. Resources for supporting missions were scarce. The Foreign Mission Board was destitute and virtually out of business because of the economic effect of the Civil War.

The mite boxes weren't filled with loose change or out of an abundance of income. They were filled by sacrifice and hard work. Catherine Allen, in her book, A *Century to Celebrate,* said, "Some women's societies organized sewing projects so that their members might earn money to contribute. In rural areas, women raised money by sale of butter, vegetables, and poultry. Most women had chickens, so eggs laid on Sunday could be sold for missions." [2] Over time, givers began to see that if you give something regularly and combine it with gifts of others, it adds up, and theirs did. It was an effective way to support missions. The idea caught on, and mite boxes found their way throughout the South and into Missouri.

As the women saw what their small gifts could do, they also realized that God could use their talents if they banded and worked together. This encouraged the expansion of Ladies Aid Societies. While some societies already had been formed, the effectiveness of the mite boxes encouraged more groups to develop. Women gathered together for long days of work in which they prepared food and clothing to be shipped to missionaries in boxes and barrels. The fruits of their labors aided many missionaries and gave women an active role in missions work around the globe.

The first documented ladies' society in Missouri was the Liberty Missionary Society, formed in 1869 at the Second Baptist Church in Liberty. In the 1870s, Female Foreign Missionary Societies that contributed to the Southern Baptist Convention (SBC) Foreign Mission Board began appearing across the state. By 1876, several statewide Southern Baptist missionary societies had been organized. These societies wanted to work together, so a meeting was held in conjunction with the Missouri Baptist General Association Convention at Hannibal in October 1876, where initial plans were made for a state missions organization.

Mr. R.S. Duncan of the Foreign Mission Board and Mrs. O.P. Moss were two pivotal nurturers involved in the creation of what would be the Missouri Baptist Woman's Missionary Society. Mr. Duncan had been busy in Missouri helping create new local woman's foreign mission societies, so he had the contacts needed to help bring the societies of the state together.

CHAPTER 1

Mrs. Moss was well-known in Missouri Baptist circles since she had served as President of the Liberty Missionary Society. She was eager to expand missions support to the state level. With the assistance of others in the state, Duncan and Moss arranged another organizational meeting which occurred April 8, 1877.

That fall, they held what was to be the first of what they would call Annual Meetings at Lexington signifying they had become an official organization. Mrs. Moss was elected President, and the society drew up a constitution to guide the new Missouri Baptist Woman's Missionary Society as an Auxiliary to the Foreign Mission Board of the Southern Baptist Convention.

The Missouri Baptist Woman's Missionary Society had grown to seventy local societies. By 1882, it was ready for organizational changes. The first was a new name: the Missouri Baptist Woman's Foreign Missionary Society. The second change followed the moving of the Missouri Baptist General Association's headquarters in 1878 to Mexico. Consequently, the women moved their offices to Mexico.

On October 15, 1923, Missouri Baptist women assembled at the First Baptist Church of Poplar Bluff. Here a lasting name was given to their work: the Woman's Missionary Union, Auxiliary to the Missouri Baptist General Association (MBGA). This became their official birthdate, but as you can see, much had happened previously to bring this about, including those little mite boxes.

While mite boxes don't have an official connection to the birth date of Missouri Woman's Missionary Union, their use shows the climate that eventually produced this organization. It also shows the caliber of women who would bring missions involvement to the forefront of Missourians and keep it there. That's why most chapters are titled by the names of particular women leaders. They were a dedicated group of women committed to supporting missions.

The Missouri Woman's Missionary Union has experienced many changes since the days of mite boxes, but the same dedication, the same resourcefulness, and the same sense of possibility still exists allowing its members to persevere through changes and challenges. You'll see this as you follow their one-hundred-year journey. You'll realize there is truly reason to celebrate.

CHAPTER 2
The Leadership of Mable Lyne Reynolds

Missouri WMU
Corresponding Secretary
1921-1936

Mable Lyne was born in 1871 on a farm near Slater to Thomas and Eliza Lyne. She spent her early years in activities at the Rehoboth Baptist Church, which later moved to Slater and became known as the First Baptist Church. After high school, she attended the Baptist Female College in Lexington and graduated in 1890. She married J.G. Reynolds in 1891, and they had a son and a daughter. Mable was active in church and the mission support programs at Slater First

Baptist Church. She also participated in the Saline Baptist Association mission programs. She served as a member of the Woman's Committee until her appointment as the first Missouri WMU Corresponding Secretary in 1921. At the time of her appointment, the family moved to Kansas City, where the Missouri Baptist headquarters were located.

Missouri Baptist women met in Jefferson City May 31-June 2, 1922. The women had not come together in a mass meeting for five years. The major item of business at this meeting was the suggestion that the women form a state Woman's Missionary Union such as those in other southern states.

The women were receptive to the idea of forming a state WMU and departed the meeting excited about a new era for woman's work. They were mindful of the success of the Woman's Committee, and the growth of missions support over the whole state. The women had a burning desire to serve God through the advancement of missions.

Mrs. Reynolds resigned from her position as corresponding secretary in December 1936, when she moved to Detroit, Michigan, to be near her children. Missouri Baptist missions support was well-established when Mrs. Reynolds left. She had carried out the wishes of Missouri WMU from its creation in 1923 on through the depression and onto a steadfast foundation in the mid-1930s. Mrs. Reynolds was

CHAPTER 1

proud of her contributions to this missions-loving organization. Mable Reynolds died in Detroit on March 23, 1954, and was buried at Forest Hill Cemetery in Kansas City.

CHAPTER 3

The Presidency of Laura Malotte Armstrong

Missouri WMU President
1923-1934

Baptist women from across Missouri gathered at First Baptist Church, Poplar Bluff, on October 15, 1923. The women voted to accept the constitution of the new Missouri Woman's Missionary Union with the objective: *"to promote Christian missions through the organization of Woman's Missionary Union in the churches of the Missouri Baptist Convention."* [1] The objective is still present; missions is the central focus of Missouri Woman's Missionary Union.

Laura Dell Malotte Armstrong was the first President of the Missouri WMU. Laura was born into

CHAPTER 3

a Baptist preacher's family in Graham, Missouri, on February 3, 1886. She was educated in public schools in northwest Missouri and attended Missouri State Teacher's College in Maryville, prior to becoming a public school teacher. She married Frank Wade Armstrong on September 4, 1907. Frank was an active Baptist layman and an attorney in Maryville. She assumed the life of a lawyer's wife in Trimble and later a judge's wife in Plattsburgh. Mrs. Armstrong was elected to the MBGA Executive Board in 1919 and served until 1936. One of her interests was student work on college campuses; she was instrumental in starting Baptist Student Union work in Missouri. Her involvement in Woman's Missionary Union included the Missouri presidency from 1923-1934.

Laura Armstrong was an able leader. She led MWMU until 1933, when she was elected President of the national WMU. Laura is the only woman from Missouri to hold that office so far. The Missouri WMU women accepted Laura's resignation with pride. In 1933, Laura was the first national WMU President elected from west of the Mississippi River. Armstrong served as national WMU as President from 1933-1945.

"Laura D. Armstrong worked her way through the WMU ranks as no other national WMU President had. For ten years, she served as an influential committee woman for national WMU. Her strongest contribution was in launching the formal stewardship education and tithing emphasis of WMU. She chaired a committee beginning in 1926, which produced the tithing record card, the tither's pin and the seal."[2]

"Armstrong was backed in her leadership by two close personal friends in WMU: Madge Nicholson Truex (Mrs. C.M.), executive secretary of Missouri WMU, and Cora Cowgill McWilliams (Mrs. George), her successor as President of Missouri WMU."[3]

The main work of Armstrong's national WMU presidency was building the WMU Training School, located adjacent to Southern Baptist Theological Seminary in Louisville, Kentucky. "The President of WMU, SBC, was automatically chairman of the trustees of the Woman's Missionary Union Training School in Louisville, KY. Armstrong gave exceptional devotion to this part of her duties. She led the way to purchase property on Lexington Road adjoining the new campus of Southern Baptist Theological Seminary. Then she gave detailed supervision to the design of the building, which was dedicated in 1941. The terrace and gardens of the building were named in her honor."[4]

Mrs. Armstrong was one of the first women to be appointed to the Executive Committee of the Southern Baptist Convention (SBC). She received that honor in 1927. In addition, Mrs. Armstrong was a member at large of the Baptist World Alliance from 1934 until 1945. "Armstrong took a lead in Baptist

CHAPTER 3

World Alliance activities. In 1934 she traveled to Berlin, where she presided over women's meetings at the Baptist World Alliance."[5]

"Armstrong was known as a judicious leader. She gained legal experience clerking for her husband after he became probate judge of Clinton County. She could remain calm, fair, and in command during tense times, such as calling the hand of the brethren for laxity in putting women on SBC boards. She represented WMU through two different sieges of Southern Baptist Convention efforts to change the status of WMU."[6]

Several of Armstrong's friends expressed concern over Laura when high blood pressure began to plague her in 1937, but responsibilities kept her on task. The national WMU Annual Meeting in 1944 was delayed because of travel limits during the war. Laura was intending to retire in 1945, but the meeting could not be held that year. Laura Armstrong suffered a cerebral hemorrhage and died on Mother's Day, May 13, 1945, at 59 years old. She was buried in Maryville, Missouri.

The state WMU scheduled Annual Meetings immediately prior to the Missouri Baptist General Association (MBGA) conventions, and the 1924 meeting was filled with reports of a good beginning for WMU. The state work had been established into three divisions in 1923, but this was expanded to six divisions in 1924 to meet the demands of the local and associational WMUs. Within the WMU program, the Baptist women of Missouri worked to expand their Sunbeam, Royal Ambassadors, Girls Auxiliary, and Young Woman's Auxiliary (YWA) work.

The Missouri Baptist General Association had been providing some aid to Baptist students who were attending state colleges. The Missouri WMU had also channeled work through college correspondents. In 1925, the Executive Board and the WMU hosted the first statewide college student conference in Mexico. From this beginning, the state Baptist Student Union program grew. The student ministry work slowed down during the depression, but it survived. Its continued growth and success are due in part to the support given by Missouri WMU.

A new youth program, the YWA House Party, made its debut in 1928. YWAs from across the state gathered for a two-day meeting in Springfield. Two hundred fifty girls attended from 42 churches. They enjoyed the activities so much that house parties became a longstanding component of Missouri's WMU program. The girls enjoyed spending the night together in learning and fellowship, even though the adult chaperones found it challenging.

A special event of 1928 was the Ruby Anniversary of the Woman's Missionary Union of the Southern Baptist Convention. The primary emphasis of the Ruby Anniversary was enlistment. Missouri women

CHAPTER 3

participated in the emphasis and worked toward state goals. Missouri WMU organized 429 new groups and raised $100,000 in gifts during the three-year effort. It was work to achieve these goals, but the women considered the effort worthy of the celebration of forty years of national WMU.

Missouri WMU women were busy with local and state activities, but they kept on supporting home and foreign missions. In 1929, the women reached a high point in missions giving when they contributed $94,183.52 to the Cooperative Program and $27,946.05 to other mission offerings. This included a record offering of $25,220.86 to the Lottie Moon Christmas Offering for foreign missions.

Missouri WMU remembers two other events in 1929. One was the crowning of Missouri's first GA queen, twelve-year-old Martha Gwen Howard of Kansas City. Missouri WMU noted this event with pride because it indicated that the churches were accepting their program and were working toward its fulfillment.

The second event of 1929 was the last Annual Meeting the WMU held in conjunction with the MBGA convention. The Missouri WMU members had decided to meet separately from the MBGA. The first separate WMU meeting was held at First Baptist Church, Marshall, in June 1930. The practice of meeting separately continues.

The early depression years were difficult, and the Missouri WMU bore its share of adversity. The mission offerings suffered because of the dire economic conditions in the state. Another cut back was in the development of new programs for the state WMU. The records indicate that the WMU was able to maintain the existing programs, but there were no funds for expanded programming. Despite these setbacks, Baptist women supported WMU and its work. Missions has always been a priority of Missouri Baptists, and the depression didn't shove missions out of the hearts of WMU women. The amount of money available for missions was less, but the people compensated by doing more praying and strengthening their personal service and community missions work.

In 1931 the annual report found the personal service chairman announcing that there had been 1,000 conversions as a result of the witnessing efforts of WMU women in Missouri. Enlistment became a central focus for the organization amid the trying times. There was not much money around, but there were women who needed Christ and who needed to be involved in missions, so Missouri WMU aimed its efforts at people.[7]

CHAPTER 4

The Presidency of Cora Cowgill McWilliams

Missouri WMU President
1934-1941

Cora Francis Cowgill McWilliams followed Laura Armstrong as the second President of MWMU. Cora Francis Cowgill was born on September 4, 1876, in Caldwell County and attended school in Hamilton. She also attended Liberty Female College in Kansas City. She married George A. McWilliams, a banker, in September 1895. Mrs. McWilliams devoted most of her adult life to WMU work.

Her state positions included WMU Training School trustee from 1923-1927, mission study chairman from 1928-1934, Missouri WMU President from 1934-1941, and Margaret Fund Chairman from

1941-1946. Mrs. McWilliams was state and SBC chairman of the WMU Golden Jubilee in 1938 and served on the national WMU survey committee in 1944, which helped revamp WMU. She was the second woman elected to the SBC Foreign Mission Board and served for seven years. Mrs. McWilliams lived a long, fruitful life until her death at age 93 on July 30, 1969.

In 1934 there were 1,884 WMU organizations in the state, including 684 WMS, 270 YWA, 219 RA, 423 GA, and 288 Sunbeam groups. Of those 1,884 organizations, 323 had been formed in 1933-1934, and 103 of the total were standard A-1. There were 72 Associational WMUs. Missouri WMU had a past and present to be proud of in the centennial year of the Missouri Baptist General Association.

CHAPTER 5

The Leadership of Madge Nicholson Truex

Missouri WMU
Executive Secretary
1937-1947

Madge Nicholson Truex became WMU Executive Secretary on February 1, 1937. With Mrs. Truex in this new position, Missouri WMU was ready to expand its missions impact. Previously, Mrs. Mable Reynolds had been WMU Corresponding Secretary from 1923-1936.

Madge Nicholson was born on June 24, 1886, in Lexington, Missouri. Her early life was spent in Lexington where she attended public school and became a member of Lexington Baptist Church. Madge attended Lexington Baptist Female College and was serving as state junior leader for Missouri Baptists when she married Chester M. Truex on December 23, 1908. Rev. Truex was a pastor and editor of the

Central Baptist newspaper. This Missouri Baptist newspaper was published from 1868-1912 in St. Louis. In December 1912, *Central Baptist* was absorbed by *Word and Way* of Missouri Baptist Convention.

Missouri WMU continued its practice of providing scholarships to young people training for Christian service at the WMU Training School, but a new scholarship was introduced in 1937 to honor Fern Gates Mangum. Fern Gates was the state's first young people's secretary, and she continued to support WMU work, especially RAs. When Mrs. Mangum died unexpectedly, her associational WMU created a scholarship at the WMU Training School for a senior student as a memorial to her. This scholarship enabled several young women to attend the Training School. The WMU Training School in Louisville was a major lateral shoot for Missouri missions support during the latter 1930s. Missouri women contributed their time, talents, energy, and money to the building campaign. Throughout this period, the women continued to aid the Training School by meeting expense appropriations, providing special gifts and memorials, and providing scholarships for Missouri students. The Training School program demanded work from its Missouri volunteers, but the women were rewarded as young women from our state attended the Training school and then went on to lives

CHAPTER 5

of Christian service around the world.

Mrs. Truex accepted the WMU executive secretary position and served in that office from 1937 until 1947. During these years, Mrs. Truex directed the state WMU work, as well as participated in national WMU work. Mrs. Madge Truex resigned as state WMU Executive Secretary on December 8, 1947. The period from 1937 to 1947 was a productive time for Missouri WMU, as all the new programs developed on the state level. Missouri WMU grew under Mrs. Truex's guidance. In 1937 there were 2,105 organizations with 32,565 members, and gifts of $59,123.60 were channeled through the state office. In 1947 there were 3,027 organizations with 46,240 members, and gifts were $364,234.24.

Mrs. Truex served well in guiding the state into new growth and service, and she also strengthened the tie between WMU and the church. Mrs. Cora McWilliams summarized Mrs. Truex's contribution to Missouri WMU as being one of public relations as she helped pastors to see the value of WMU. The Truex years were honorable to God, as were the preceding years of Missouri missions support. With faith that God would provide another leader, the women of WMU marched on into the future with hearts full of love and lives willing to serve. Madge N. Truex died on December 30, 1961.

CHAPTER 6

The Presidency of Louise Enloe McKee

Missouri WMU President
1941-1946

Mrs. Cora McWilliams stepped down from the presidency in 1941 after serving for seven years. Louise Enloe McKee was elected as the third President at the WMU Annual Meeting in April 1941 at Second Baptist Church, St. Louis.

Louise Enloe was born in Russellville on February 22, 1897. She united with Russellville Baptist Church in 1909 and continued her Christian training at Hardin Junior College in Mexico, Missouri, from 1913-1917. She graduated from Central Missouri State University in 1925 and had a long career as a home economics teacher. On June 7, 1930, she married

CHAPTER 6

Thomas W. McKee in New Bloomfield. Mrs. McKee was active in the Providence Church in Callaway Association, where she worked with RAs. She served as state WMU Stewardship chairman from 1937 until she was elected state WMU President in 1941.

Following her five years as WMU President, she served in other state offices, including Business Woman's Circle advisor, Vice-President for night circles, and interim Executive Secretary. Mrs. McKee led Missouri WMU through the trying period of World War II. Many plans were altered because of the war, but Missouri women continued to emphasize missions under the leadership of Mrs. McKee, Mrs. Truex, and other state staff members.

Mrs. McKee recalls that one of the most rewarding and beneficial efforts of her presidency was the work she did with the divisional meetings. In the fall of each year, she and Mrs. Truex would divide the state in half so that one would cover thirteen divisional meetings in the northern half while the other would cover thirteen meetings in the southern half. For about two weeks, the workers traveled the state, spreading the mission story. Divisional meetings were some of the most popular events during the war years.

A year of adjustments for Missouri WMU was 1943 when the country was in the height of World War II. Most of the changes came about because of wartime rationing and restrictions. YWA House

Parties were not held because of the difficulties in transportation. Other programs had to be canceled or curtailed, but the women remained devoted in their support of missions. Work continued on the local, association, divisional, and state levels; and the women did the best they could considering the circumstances.

A Missouri WMU Annual Meeting was not held in 1945 because of the war, but the women remained active in supporting missions. In 1945, eight interracial institutes were held across Missouri. Missouri WMU women participated in the institutes to help African-American Baptist women develop missions organizations. The women met together to discuss better methods of promoting mission programs.

Mrs. McKee ended her tenure as President of Missouri WMU in the spring of 1946. Mrs. McKee's resignation was accepted with regret. She had led the Woman's Missionary Union through the war years and promoted three of her major interests: the small church WMU, stewardship, and Royal Ambassadors.

CHAPTER 7
The Presidency of Josephine Riley Medlin

Missouri WMU President
1946

Josephine Riley Medlin became Missouri WMU's fourth President when she succeeded Mrs. Louise McKee.

Josephine Franklin Riley was born to Albert and Ida Riley on February 22, 1907, in El Dorado, Arkansas. While a youth, she joined the First Baptist Church of El Dorado and was active in its work. She graduated from Ouachita Baptist University and the WMU Training School in Louisville. Her association with Missouri WMU began in 1932 when she became young people's secretary. She served in that position until she married T. Shad Medlin on June 21, 1934.

While Mr. Medlin was serving in the military during World War II, Josephine Medlin served as young people's secretary from 1944-1945. She was elected state WMU President in April 1946 and served only a few months. She resigned that fall when her husband was transferred to Richmond, Virginia. Josephine Medlin died in 1966 and was buried in El Dorado, Arkansas.

Two new major programs were instituted during Mrs. Medlin's tenure. Both programs are related to the state Baptist Assembly at Hollister. Hollister became the Missouri Baptist Assembly in 1945, and WMU women found the facilities inviting. The first WMU Conference was held at Hollister in 1946. Women from across the state came to the Ozarks for some relaxation, Christian fellowship, and intensive missions training. The conferences were very successful.

CHAPTER 8

The Presidency of LeeAnna Floy Kinell

Missouri WMU President
1946-1952

When Mrs. Medlin left in the fall of 1946, Mrs. LeeAnna Floy Kinell was elected as the fifth state WMU President.

LeeAnna Floy was born on November 22, 1894. She married Fred B. Kinell and assumed the role of pastor's wife and mother to their children. Mrs. Kinell supported WMU work through her entire adult life. On the state level, she was chairman of Division Nine from 1925-1931 and chairman of the St. Joseph Division from 1932-1941. Mrs. Kinell became state WMU Vice-President in 1941 and served in that capacity until her election as President in 1946.

Shortly after Mrs. Kinell became President, she received good news to share with Missouri women. The national WMU had notified LeeAnna that Missouri was ranked first in mission study awards for 1945-1946. This honor was an indication that Missouri women were strong supporters of mission study. Her presidency ended in 1952 when she had served her five-year term limit. Mrs. Kinell was the author of a historical booklet on Missouri WMU in 1963.

Mrs. Kinell went early to the Wednesday prayer meeting at her church located in Savannah, Missouri, on November 2, 1972, to spend time alone in prayer. When church members arrived, they found that Mrs. Kinell had passed on to be with the Lord. She was buried in Webb City, Missouri.

CHAPTER 9
The Leadership of Eva Berry

Missouri WMU
Executive Secretary
1947-1954

The years 1948-1954 were a time of transition for Missouri Baptists, including the WMU. The war years were over, and Missouri Baptists were ready to move on into areas of expanded ministry. The headquarters for the Missouri Baptist General Association had been located in Kansas City. In 1947 they relocated the headquarters to Jefferson City because it was more centrally located. The move caused some distress to the WMU and was a factor in the Executive Secretary's resignation in December 1947. Madge Truex remained in Kansas City, and her former field secretary, Eva Berry, assumed the job of Executive Secretary.

Eva Berry was born in Alabama. She graduated from Wheeler Business College and Howard College in Birmingham and was a 1932 graduate of the WMU Training School in Louisville, Kentucky. Eva was the state WMU Young People's Secretary of Alabama for nine years and was field secretary of Birmingham Baptist WMU for one year. Miss Berry came to Missouri in 1944 as a field worker in the WMU and served in that position until she became Executive Secretary in 1947. Berry guided the WMU office until she resigned in April 1954. Eva later served as executive secretary of WMU in the Kansas Baptist Convention. She died on June 1, 1957, following an auto accident while she was promoting WMU work in Iowa.

One key event of 1948 was the organization of the Missouri Baptist Business Woman's Federation. The number of local Business Woman's Circles (BWC) had grown since their creation in Springfield in 1937, so it was natural for these groups to form a state organization. The women met prior to the April 1948 state WMU meeting and chose Miss Dorothy Meyer as President. In June 1948, Mrs. Paul Weber was elected state BWC advisor. Under the leadership of these two women, Business Woman's Circles grew in their involvement in missions work.

CHAPTER 9

In 1948 two long-term workers came to help Eva Berry. The workers were Mary Bidstrup, who came as state field secretary to create new WMUs and aid local groups in enlistment and enlargement. The second worker was Anna Belle Crouch, who assumed the position of young people's secretary. These well-trained and dedicated women helped Miss Berry guide all phases of the state WMU work.

By midsummer of 1949, the WMU had a new state office in Jefferson City, and the women were ready to devote full attention to new areas of missions support. One project, initiated in August 1949, was the writing of the state WMU history. Missouri WMU asked Mrs. Cora McWilliams to write the history, and she began the task of compiling the material on organized Baptist Woman's missionary activity in Missouri.

The 1950s began with a busy year for the women. The state staff of Eva Berry, Anna Belle Crouch, and Mary Bidstrup provided the guidance needed for the ongoing programs. Mrs. Kinell directed the women as President, and many programs continued in popularity and support. Missouri was well-represented at the WMU Training School with ten young women attending. Other Missouri women were preparing for missions at New Orleans Seminary and Southwestern Seminary.

The new decade was off to a strong start in the 1950s. WMU work on the associational and local levels was prospering. The 1950 annual report states that there were 3,592 organizations with 52,558 members in Missouri.

Work with African-American women and youth was a major emphasis of the 1950s. The Interracial Institutes remained a beneficial training ground for African-American women. Some local WMUs were fostering cooperation between African-Americans and white Baptist women through local cooperative councils. Missouri Baptist women decided to create the Interracial Missouri Baptist Woman's Missionary Council in 1950. This council provided opportunities for Baptist women of different denominations to send representatives to meetings where cooperative endeavors were planned.

Missouri WMU was proud to present its first published history in 1951, in conjunction with the 75th anniversary of the beginning of Baptist woman's work in Missouri. Mrs. Cora McWilliams chronicled the exciting work of Missouri Baptist women in her book, *Women and Missions*. The Diamond Jubilee Annual Meeting was held in Kansas City on April 5-6, 1951, with 2,700 people in attendance. The highlight of the meeting was the presentation of a historical pageant depicting the years of women's missions support in Missouri.

The country was engulfed in the Korean War from 1950-1953. The Korean Conflict made Missouri's

CHAPTER 9

women more aware of the people of the world and the need for better communication and goodwill. Missouri WMU worked toward this goal in its own backyard in 1951 when it contributed to the work of Mrs. Fred Neiger at the University of Missouri Baptist Student Union in Columbia. Mrs. Neiger received $25 to aid in her work with international students and their families at the MU campus. This began a new avenue of missions support for WMU women, as they reached out to the international students who were temporary residents in Missouri.

The 1952 Annual Meeting of Missouri WMU was a session for changing the state's WMU structure. One of the changes was the elimination of the divisions. The divisions had been a useful part of the WMU program since 1923, but it was becoming more difficult to find women to serve as chairmen. The divisional meetings had been well-attended, but the consensus was that the divisional framework should be eliminated.

Another new provision was to have the term of state officers limited to five years. This allowed the officers a chance to serve and develop their ideas, but it also allowed for a continual change that brought in new women to serve.

The final change was the creation of the WMU Specials Fund and an offering with the same name. The Specials Fund became an inclusive designation for contributions to the Burney Fund, MWMU Training School, nurse's scholarship, Training School scholarships, work with African-American Baptists, magazines for Missouri missionaries, and the national WMU Building Fund.

CHAPTER 10

The Presidency of Lena Shaner Burnham

Missouri WMU President
1952-1956

At the 1952 Annual Meeting, Mrs. Lena Burnham was elected the sixth President of the Missouri Woman's Missionary Union.

Lena Pearl Shaner was born at Hazel Run on November 18, 1899, to Rev. and Mrs. George Shaner. She was raised in a Christian home and joined the Leadwood Baptist Church at age thirteen. Following a public-school education, Lena attended Will Mayfield College in Marble Hill. She married Rev. O.R. Burnham on June 26, 1928 in St. Louis. Her life was filled with the responsibilities of being a preacher's wife and the mother of their son. Her involvement in state WMU work began in 1947 when she served as mission study chairman. She was BWC representative in 1950 and was elected WMU state President in 1952, serving in that position until 1956. Mrs. Burnham was also an active national WMU Vice-President and served on several pivotal SBC committees.

Mrs. Burnham began her tenure as President by assuring the implementation of the new WMU constitution and continuing work with the African-American Baptist Women. Missouri WMU leaders saw work with African-American Baptist women as a vital aspect of missions support. A Baptist Woman's Leadership Conference was held at Hollister in 1952, which focused on better training for all Baptist women and the improvement of relationships between African-American and white Southern Baptist women.

In 1953, new changes were taking place. Missouri students were still being educated at the WMU Training School, although the name had been changed to the Carver School of Missions and Social Work. Guidelines were expanded to award scholarships to women students attending Southern Baptist seminaries in addition to those attending Carver School. Another change took place when the Specials Fund was renamed the Madge N. Truex Fund in recognition of the contributions made by Mrs. Truex through the years.

CHAPTER 10

Three major events took place in 1954, which had an impact on the work of Missouri WMU. The first of these was the U.S. Supreme Court ruling on integration. This decision legally opened up new avenues of freedom for the nation's African-American population. The Missouri WMU continued its support of African-American Baptist women's work and the Missouri Baptist Woman's Council. Young African-American women were encouraged to attend national Young Women's Auxiliary (NYWAs) Conferences.

The other two major events of 1954 dealt with Missouri Baptist actions. Earl Harding was selected as Executive Secretary of the Missouri Baptist General Association, and Southern Baptist work was begun in Iowa. Missouri WMU staff introduced WMU work to the Iowa women by conducting meetings and workshops.

Missouri WMU realized that there had been and were a multitude of missionaries from the state. Mrs. Ed Walsh began work in 1954 to compile biographies of these missionaries so that a book could be written about Missouri missionaries.

Mrs. Burnham's service as Missouri WMU President came to an end in April 1956. Mrs. Burnham had brought innovations and strong leadership to her position.

CHAPTER 11

The Leadership of Hilda Beggs

Missouri WMU
Executive Secretary
1954-1958

During the spring of 1954, several personnel changes occurred in the WMU staff. Eva Berry and Anna Belle Crouch resigned from their positions. This left Mary Bidstrup and Willis Griffin as the two staff members. Mrs. T.W. McKee, former WMU President, was asked to serve as the interim executive secretary during the summer months until she had to return to her teaching position in the fall.

Mary Bidstrup served as acting Executive Secretary through the fall months in addition to her

CHAPTER 11

other duties. Mrs. A.B. Constantz joined the staff in August of 1954 as field secretary, and Jane Averitt took over as young people's secretary. In December, Hilda Beggs became the executive secretary, with Mary Bidstrup serving as assistant executive secretary. Once again, the office staff was complete.

Hilda Beggs was born in Macon, Georgia. She graduated from Mercer University and the Carver School of Missions and Social Work. Miss Beggs worked as an educational director in three churches in Georgia and South Carolina. Her WMU experience came from over six years of service as field secretary for the Georgia WMU. Miss Beggs served as executive secretary of the Missouri WMU from December 1954 until 1958, when she returned to Florida.

By 1955, Missouri WMU had become a sizeable organization. The records for that year indicate there were 5,341 organizations comprised of 1,372 women's societies and 3,969 young people's organizations. The WMU membership totaled 75,997.

National WMU had been in the process of change since the early 1940s. Missouri's own Laura Armstrong (national WMU President 1933-1945) began this process when she appointed a Survey Committee. Slowly changes were made, and the face of national WMU was altered with the prayer that the organization would be better and stronger. As national WMU changed, Missouri WMU tried to adapt so that the state programs would be in line with national programs.

One of the first changes because of national WMU revisions was in program structure. Missouri WMU endorsed this new structure and urged associational and local unions to accept it. In order to encourage the new terminology, the position of field secretary at the state office was changed to Secretary of Fundamentals. Nell Constantz assumed this new title and worked across the state to emphasize the value of prayer, mission study, stewardship, and community missions. Jane Averitt worked with the restructured Youth Department.

Publications were a focus of Missouri WMU work in 1955. The Quarterly Bulletin and the Missouri WMU Handbook were instituted. Mrs. Burnham saw the need for improved communication for the WMU women of the state. It was thought that a special WMU newsletter would help get publicity and information out to the women. The Missouri WMU Handbook provided statistics, directory information, a calendar of activities, and information on recommended local and associational structure. Yearly supplements updated the material in the handbook.

While national WMU and Missouri WMU leadership were effecting changes in the Missouri WMU, the Missouri Baptist General Association (MBGA) joined

CHAPTER 11

in the process of trying to make the organization more efficient and effective. The major action they took toward the WMU was the inclusion of WMU as a department of the MBGA in 1955. Cautiously the women moved into this new relationship. The WMU began functioning as the only MBGA department which also had an independent membership and organizational structure. It was a time of learning, but everyone diligently worked to make the new relationship viable. After becoming a department of work, Missouri WMU achieved its closest unity with the MBGA.

One adjustment which was made to reflect the departmental status of WMU was the alteration of their constitution into bylaws. Once the bylaws were approved and accepted, a new policy manual was written to make clear all the new procedures and relationships which were part of Missouri WMU.

CHAPTER 12

The Presidency of Elizabeth Tillery Crozier

Missouri WMU President
1956-1960

Martha Elizabeth Tillery was born to Orla and Loretta Tillery on June 29, 1911, in Kansas City. Elizabeth was raised in a Christian home and accepted Christ at the age of fourteen. She graduated from Flemington high school and attended Southwest Missouri State University in Springfield, Moark College in West Plains, and Southwest Baptist College in Bolivar. She married Leonard Crozier on April 11, 1931, and the couple had two children. Mrs. Crozier was active in her church in West Plains and especially in WMU work. She was elected President of Missouri

CHAPTER 12

WMU in 1956 at the Annual Meeting in Carthage, and served in that position until 1960. Elizabeth served as Missouri Vice-President of national WMU and was involved in the transitions taking place at the state and national levels.

One of Mrs. Crozier's first tasks was to oversee the national WMU inspired transition from the Standards of Excellence to the Aims for Advancement. National WMU felt that local WMUs had become too engrossed with meeting the specific requirements of the Standards of Excellence and that the spirit of missions support had been lost along the way. The Aims for Advancement were designed to be a more flexible guide that would allow options for the various local unions and stress spiritual development. Mrs. Crozier and the state office staff had the task of acquainting the Missouri women with new Aims and encouraging their usage.

A new item for 1956 was a Queens' Court at the state GA camp. This provided an opportunity for the girls who had achieved the rank of Queen to be recognized for their work, and Queens' Court acted as an extra boost to encourage girls to attend camp.

Also occurring in 1956 was the transfer of the RA secretary, Willis Griffin, from the WMU Department to the Brotherhood. Mrs. Ed Walsh completed her missionary biography collection, *Assignment: Light Bearers, in 1956.* It became yet another useful mission support tool generated through the state WMU. The Missouri Baptist General Association made a decision in 1956 to purchase property located near Roach, MO, on Lake of the Ozarks. This property became known as Windermere Baptist Assembly.

Throughout 1957, the Missouri WMU officers and staff worked to adapt to the changes taking place due to the decisions made by MBGA, national WMU, and Missouri WMU. Bernice Scrivner and Helen Stacy served as secretaries in the WMU, and they died in an accident on the way to the WMU Annual Meeting in April 1957. Missouri Baptists were shocked and saddened by their sudden deaths. WMU work continued, but Bernice and Helen were missed by all who had known and worked with them. The Missouri WMU Executive Committee decided to honor their memory by donating $500 to the well project in New Mexico in 1958. It was fitting that a source of new water was created in memory of two ladies who served the Master of the living water.

Two actions of the WMU Executive Committee in 1957 involved African-American Baptists. The first was the sponsoring of an African-American Youth Camp at Hollister. The WMU worked closely with African-American Baptist women's groups to establish a camp that was enjoyed by all those who participated. The other action was an invitation by the WMU for African-American Baptist women to attend

CHAPTER 12

the WMU Annual Conference held in Hollister.

Hilda Beggs, the Executive Secretary, resigned at the end of 1958. The work continued under the guidance of President Crozier and the office staff of Bidstrup, White, and Constantz. More changes were in store for Missouri WMU, but by now, the women were accustomed to change, and acceptance came much easier.

Besides changes within Missouri and national WMU, there was a changing world to deal with in 1958. Women's priorities and lifestyles were changing, and this had an impact on WMU. These many changes were difficult for the Missouri Baptist Women to absorb. Some women opted for a new lifestyle which included work outside the home, and they dropped out of WMU. But Missouri WMU survived because of the women who remained faithful to Baptist mission support regardless of the changes going on around them. These women became the core of the "new WMU," and they led their friends into brighter days for Missouri WMU.

The next year of Missouri WMU work was one filled with celebrations. It was a time to celebrate the harvest of Baptist work in the nation and the state. National WMU had their share of celebrations, too, for missions support work had produced much fruit.

During 1959, Missouri Baptists celebrated 125 years as a state Baptist association. The newly named

Missouri Baptist Convention had a joyous birthday as members looked back over the triumphs and trials that had happened since 1834. Missouri WMU took pride in knowing that they had a part in this grand heritage. This was an important year for the convention, and it was also a vital year in WMU work.

CHAPTER 13

The Leadership of Mary O. Bidstrup

Missouri WMU
Executive Secretary
1959-1973

The chief event of 1959 was the selection of Mary Bidstrup as executive secretary of the Missouri WMU. Miss Bidstrup had been a devoted worker in the WMU Department since 1948.

Mary O. Bidstrup was born on August 31, 1907, to Mr. and Mrs. G.H. Bidstrup of Beaman. Mary was raised in a Christian home and accepted Christ at age sixteen at the Lamine Baptist Church in Cooper County. She graduated from Pilot Grove high school and went on to earn a Bachelor's Degree in education from Central Missouri State University, Warrensburg. Following an eighteen-year career as a teacher, Miss

Bidstrup earned a Master's Degree in Religious Education from Southwestern Baptist Theological Seminary. Miss Bidstrup began work with Missouri WMU on June 1, 1948, as field secretary. Prior to becoming executive secretary, she was assistant to the executive secretary. Miss Bidstrup served as executive secretary until June 1, 1973. Altogether, Miss Bidstrup worked with Missouri WMU for twenty-five years.

Missouri WMU had stability when it entered the Bidstrup era. Mrs. Crozier had two years of experience and wisdom as state President. The WMU volunteers on the state, associational, and local levels were committed to missions. The WMU staff of Nell Constantz and Ashley White were confident in their abilities as age group leaders. This stability was important because the national WMU was continuing its restructuring. Part of the restructuring process was changing the titles of the workers. In order to match the structure of the national WMU, the Missouri WMU staff received new titles. Miss Bidstrup remained Executive Secretary, and Nell Constantz became the Woman's Missionary Society (WMS) Director, Ashley White became YWA and Sunbeam Director, and Bobbie Sorrill joined the staff as GA Director. The new designations made clear the responsibilities of the staff members, and there was little resistance to this change.

CHAPTER 13

Another change in the WMU structure came about in late 1959 when the Business Woman's Federation merged with the WMU and became the Association of Night Circles of Missouri. The local and state Business Woman's organizations were an important part of the missions support program in Missouri. These groups gave working women an opportunity to participate in missions and to have programming unique to their interests. As with previous name changes for Missouri Baptist Woman's Missionary organizations, the work continued, although the name was new.

A significant event in 1959 was when Windermere Baptist Assembly officially opened. The women were thrilled to have a centrally located conference center, and many meetings were held there. Windermere became an integral part of the WMU program as the Business Woman's Circles (BWC) Conference, the YWA Conference, and the first state WMU Assembly was held there. Camp Windermere for Girls was founded in 1959. Over 350 girls participated in the new camp program in 1959.

Another new creation for 1959 was associational GA councils. Many associations in the state sponsored quarterly gatherings of GAs. Another GA gathering which was successful was the GA Queens' Court. All girls who had achieved the step of Queen or higher were eligible to attend a special two-day meeting. The response was so great that the event had to be limited to Intermediate GAs in subsequent years. Because of the GAs enthusiastic response to associational GA councils and Queens' Court, it was evident that the traditions were going to endure.

Missouri WMU sponsored its first bus trip to Ridgecrest for WMU ladies in 1959. For many years, the state had sent YWAs to the national YWA conference. This was the first time for a busload of WMS ladies to attend a national conference. The response was good, and another tradition was begun.

A final noteworthy event for 1959 was the beginning of the national WMU emphasis on Aims for Advancement. The associations in Missouri adopted new Associational Aims for Advancement to be used as a measuring tool for the success of the total WMU program. Missouri WMU realized the value of setting goals, and the Associational Aims for Advancement was yet another goal to be reached.

The decade of the 1960s opened brightly for Missouri WMU. A trained office staff implemented the plans made by the dedicated WMU Executive Committee. Almost 73,000 women and children were involved in mission support at the associational and local levels. Many young women were in the Carver School, SBC seminaries, and schools of nursing, preparing for full-time Christian service. Traditional programs received continued acceptance, and new programs were embraced wholeheartedly.

CHAPTER 14

The Presidency of Eunice Powell Allison

Missouri WMU President
1960-1964

Springtime in 1960 brought some Woman's Missionary Union personnel changes. Mrs. Crozier declined renomination as state WMU President, so a new President had to be found. The nominating committee presented the name of Mrs. Bradley Allison at the Annual Meeting, and the women welcomed her.

Eunice K. Powell was born in Kaufman, Texas, on September 6, 1912. Her parents were Rhena and Needham Powell. She was raised in Kaufman and accepted Christ at age twelve at Kaufman First Baptist Church. Following high school graduation, she attended Howard Payne College, where she received her Bachelor of Arts degree. While attending Howard

Payne, she married Rev. Bradley Allison on May 28, 1932. Mrs. Allison was active as a mother of three sons, a preacher's wife, and a WMU member. She was involved in WMU work on all levels and served as mission study director for Missouri WMU in the 1950s. In addition to her state work, she wrote articles for *Royal Service* and served as Vice-President, representing Missouri on the national WMU board. Mrs. Allison was an active leader in the 75th Anniversary celebration in 1963 of national WMU. She served as state WMU President from 1960 until 1964.

The main emphasis of 1960 for Missouri WMU was to get settled in at Windermere. Many of the conferences and camps had been moved to that new facility in 1959, so there was a push to encourage women and children to attend the meetings. Another Windermere project was the proposed Children's Building. The WMU Executive Committee donated over $2,000 to the Children's Building project. The WMU women realized that child care would be an asset in enticing women to attend conferences at Windermere. Having a nice facility for children would provide an opportunity to educate the babies and preschoolers who would be at Windermere with their mothers.

WMU Week changed its format in 1960 because of the large number of women attending the meeting at Windermere. For the first time, there were three

CHAPTER 14

complete sessions of WMU Week to allow a maximum number of members to attend.

The WMU women wanted to have a complete office staff. Martha Fellows came to join the staff as the YWA/Sunbeam Director. With the staff once again complete, it was easier to implement the plans of the Executive Committee. The women had a vision of a brighter future, and they were ready to proceed with vigor.

A committee was appointed to reactivate the Missouri Baptist Woman's Missionary Council in May 1961. This committee consisted of five African-American and five white Baptist women. The ladies worked closely with the Department for Work with national Baptists and prepared to reorganize the council in 1962.

The youngest members of the WMU program enjoyed 1961 because it was the 75th anniversary celebration for the Sunbeam Band. National WMU met in St. Louis in 1961, so some Missouri children were able to take part in the Sunbeam anniversary festivities. The highlight for state activities was a Sunbeam Band Anniversary party held jointly with the Association of Night Circles at the Missouri WMU Annual Meeting in Columbia. Several hundred of the 13,176 Missouri Sunbeam members came to the party, and it was a memorable event in their lives.

Other statewide meetings for 1961 included WMU Week at Windermere, Camp Windermere for Girls,

YWA Conference, YWA House Parties, and the first Advanced Leadership Training Course at Windermere, which emphasized camping. It was a year for study and learning, some of the favorite activities of Missouri WMU women.

In 1962, the GAs of Missouri celebrated the 50th anniversary of their organization. Special activities were enjoyed by the 14,991 girls enrolled in Missouri GA groups. Many girls attended the special festivities at the Annual Meeting in Springfield. All of this took place while the GA Director position was changing. Bobbie Sorrill left Missouri in 1962. She was succeeded by Rosetta McIntire, who had a solid start in her work because of the special attention given to the 50th anniversary of GA activities.

The biggest WMU celebration of the 1960s took place in 1963 when national WMU recognized its 75th anniversary. Missouri had a special part in this because the meeting was held in Kansas City. Those women at the meeting count it as one of the most memorable they have attended. Missouri WMU also did some celebrating on their own. The foremost activity was the WMU Annual Meeting held in St. Louis. Missionaries and national WMU personnel highlighted the meeting, and Missouri WMU women participated in various ways. Former state WMU Presidents and the granddaughter of Mrs. S.Y. Pitts captivated the audience with their memories. Other special activities included an anniversary tea and

CHAPTER 14

pageant. Mrs. Fred Kinell wrote a booklet entitled *A Supplement to Women and Missions in Missouri 1951-1963*. It was a festive year for the 70,862 members and 4,910 organizations across the state.

In addition to the anniversary festivities and the traditional activities, two new programs were introduced to the Missouri WMU in 1963. Mrs. T.W. McKee attended the Convention Literacy Workshop and demonstrated the literacy work plan at the State WMU Conference at Windermere. This began another program that Missouri WMU could use to minister to those around them with special needs. The second new program was the first Baptist Women's Day of Prayer Around the World which was observed in November. Missouri Baptist women gained strength in knowing that their prayers were united with those of Baptist women in the rest of the world as all prayed for the fulfillment of the Great Commission.

Missouri WMU was proud of its success in its Jubilee goals in 1964. The following goals were achieved: net gain of 7,500 members, increases in Cooperative Program gifts, increases in Lottie Moon Offering, increases in WMU magazine subscriptions by 75, increases in YWA and GA membership, increases in the number of Honor WMUs, presentation of Jubilee goals in associational quarterly meetings, three Advanced Leadership Training meetings, and promotion of Aims Books.

CHAPTER 15

The Presidency of Ferroll Woodford Delozier

Missouri WMU President
1964-1969

In 1964, Eunice Allison declined to be nominated for a fifth year. Mrs. Ferroll DeLozier assumed the presidency following her election by the state WMU members in 1964 at the Annual Meeting at First Baptist Church, St. Joseph.

Ferroll Lucile Woodford was born on September 17, 1908, at Osceola, Missouri to Mr. and Mrs. I.W. Woodford. She accepted Christ at eleven years of age at the Humansville Baptist Church. She married Homer E. DeLozier at Humansville Baptist Church on May 27, 1929. Mrs. DeLozier was educated in public schools and earned a degree in music education from

CHAPTER 15

Southwest Baptist College in Bolivar. Later, she earned a Master's Degree in Religious Education from Central Baptist Seminary in Kansas City. Dr. and Mrs. DeLozier had two daughters. Mrs. DeLozier spent her time caring for her family and serving her local church and association. Since Dr. DeLozier was Executive Director of the St. Louis Baptist Association, Mrs. DeLozier worked with WMUs in her association. Mrs. DeLozier concentrated her WMU work on GAs and YWAs. She became a member of the Executive Committee in 1958 and served as Missouri WMU Vice-President for several years. During the time she served as state President, she was active in the work of reorganization at the national level. Mrs. DeLozier served as President of Missouri WMU and led the state until 1969, when her five-year term ended. Mrs. DeLozier passed away in April 1993 at the age of 84.

A special emphasis for the summer of 1964 was Sunbeam work which was carried out by a summer Sunbeam worker, Bertha Wright. Her summer was filled with work to strengthen Sunbeam Bands. One of her major programs was a series of twelve Sunbeam Band Day Camping Clinics. The work of the summer Sunbeam worker was well-accepted, so it continued until a full-time Sunbeam Director was hired.

Another special program of 1964 was a State Literacy Workshop to train women to carry out this vital work in their own communities. The Madge

Truex Fund was adjusted so that YWA members could donate to the worthy fund. This adjustment enlarged the giving base, which was needed to achieve the 1964 goal of $12,300. To show support of the Civil Rights Act passed by Congress in 1964, the WMU Executive Committee announced that it would continue a policy of not barring anyone from meetings because of race.

Missouri WMU continued to carry out its programs in 1964. Meanwhile, national WMU was involved in a massive reevaluation of its purpose within the Southern Baptist Convention. In 1963 WMU had agreed to participate in a convention-wide "program statement" procedure. The idea behind this was to coordinate all the activities of the various SBC boards and agencies so that there would be unity in the convention's programs. National WMU began this procedure in 1964, and it slowly had an impact on the entire nature of the organization. New concepts were passed on to the state, associational, and local levels for their consideration and implementation. Since the Missouri WMU President served as Vice-President on the national board, Missouri WMU was aware of this process. A watchful eye was kept on the happenings in Birmingham while the state staff of Bidstrup, Constantz, Fellows, and McIntire carried out the plans of the Missouri WMU Executive Committee.

One concept which originated with national WMU and filtered down to Missouri WMU was mission action. This term, which appeared in 1965, was to replace community missions. It was a description of a lifestyle to be carried out by WMU members rather than just an allotment of time for specific causes. It took a while for members to switch their terminology, but follow-up by national WMU has guaranteed that the word and the concept are part of the present WMU.

The first Area Clinics were held in 1965 at twenty-four different locations and provided in-depth training for local WMU work. The clinics were well-received, so they became an annual Missouri WMU event. Missouri WMU work progressed smoothly through the mid-sixties. The office staff, summer workers, and volunteers at the state level ensured that the traditional programs continued. Some programs expanded while others remained the same or declined in size.

One program which grew was Camp Windermere for Girls. In 1959, the program began with two GA camps and one YWA Conference. By 1966, there were five GA camps and one YWA Conference. The interest in GA camps would continue to grow in the sixties while the YWA conference would decline. Younger children were catching missions support fever, and this was to be applauded because these children hopefully would keep their missions zeal throughout their lives and remain active in WMU programs.

An action of national WMU in 1966 which interested Missouri WMU members was the appointment of Betty Bock as Young Woman's Auxiliary Director. Bock was a native of Slater, Missouri. She had been active in WMU auxiliaries all her life and had served as a Missouri WMU summer camp worker during her years at Southwestern Seminary. Missouri WMU did not have the opportunity to use her in a full-time capacity. The women who knew Betty were glad that national WMU was utilizing this dedicated Christian worker. Betty served at national WMU until 1969, when she moved on to another area of Christian service.

Missouri WMU was sad to learn of the resignation of two of its staff in 1967. Martha Fellows, who later married Rev. Ronald Robinson, resigned her position of YWA/Sunbeam director to serve on the Indiana WMU staff. Her six years of service to Missouri WMU were valuable ones, and her successor continued the tradition of longtime service. Rosetta McIntire was the other worker to leave in 1967; she resigned to become Sunbeam Band director in Alabama. Rosetta later married Dr. Jerry Bedsole and served with him as an IMB missionary.

Alberta Gilpin came to Missouri WMU in June of 1967 as YWA/Sunbeam Director. Beverly Goss, who was acquainted with Missouri GA work through her summer camp work, came to work in June of 1967, so

CHAPTER 15

the office staff was once again complete. The Missouri WMU programming continued through 1967 as in the past.

The Missouri WMU members were busy in 1968 with new programs and new changes in structure. One new program was the first GA Galaxy which was held in Bolivar in August. The Executive Committee had eliminated the Junior GA Queens' Days in the spring of 1968, so the GAs were excited to learn of the new program, which would allow all girls to attend regardless of their Forward Step achievement. GAs were so active in their organization that Camp Windermere for Girls was expanded to six weeks. The GA Galaxy gave them another opportunity to learn about missions.

There were three minor changes in structure. The first two dealt with name changes of Missouri WMU publications. In the spring of 1968, the WMU Executive Committee agreed to change the name of the *Quarterly Bulletin* to *Missouri WMU News*. They also changed the name of the *Missouri WMU Handbook* to *Missouri WMU Facts and Features*. These title changes were made to reflect a change in emphasis in the publications and to reveal more clearly the contents of the items.

A third change for 1968 was a change in organizational plans for local WMUs handed down from national WMU. These changes responded to the

SBC coordination efforts and to the changing lifestyle of American women. The new plan established the WMU as the main organization and the Woman's Missionary Society as the adult women's group. The head of the WMU was to be called director, and she was to supervise missions support work for the entire church. There were fewer officers in the new plan; it was hoped that this would free women to become more involved in churchwide missions support programs. Within the WMU, there was a change from circles to groups which were to be organized according to purpose instead of age. There were to be mission study groups, mission action groups, and prayer groups. The Missouri WMU was excited to announce the hiring of Adele Branson as a Sunbeam worker on June 1, 1968. The women across the state were enthusiastic about having a separate worker for Sunbeam Bands. This would increase emphasis on Sunbeams, and it would free some of Alberta Gilpin's time since she had previously worked with both YWAs and Sunbeams.

As with all changes in the past, some women accepted them readily, while others were more hesitant. These changes came about because national WMU felt that something had to be done to control the steady drop in membership. This was evident in Missouri since the WMU membership in 1963 was 74,203, and the 1968 membership had decreased to

CHAPTER 15

71,124. It was hoped that the proposed changes would reverse this trend and bring brighter days to WMU by involving more women and children in missions. Missouri WMU revamped its statement of policy in 1969 to reflect the new organizational plan suggested by national WMU.

CHAPTER 16

The Presidency of Viola Volkart Scherff

Missouri WMU President
1969-1974

When Mrs. DeLozier had served the limit of her term as President, the nominating committee presented Viola Scherff as the next President. Viola was elected at the Annual Meeting at First Baptist Church, Springfield, in 1969.

Viola Volkart was born in Cooper County, on November 6, 1917, to Mr. and Mrs. Walter Volkart. She united with the First Baptist Church in California at age 12 and began her life of Christian service. Viola attended public schools and later attended Central Missouri State Teachers University. She married Hughes Scherff in 1937 in Camdenton, and a son was

CHAPTER 16

born to the union. Mrs. Scherff spent most of her adult life near Clarksburg, where she was involved with her family and local church. She served in associational and local WMU offices before becoming state WMU Vice-President in 1965.

Her main interest in WMU work was with WMS, although she also served in other areas as requested. While WMU President, Mrs. Scherff was active on the national level and participated on many important committees. Mrs. Scherff served as Missouri WMU President until her term expired in 1974. Her post-presidency period was filled with WMU activity, which included writing the booklet, *A Mission of Love Through a Together Ministry – The Historical Review of Baptist Woman's Missionary Council of Missouri.* Viola Scherff passed away on June 21, 2010.

National WMU introduced a new framework in 1970, and although the change was not to take effect until October of that year, it was introduced and discussed throughout the year. It revamped WMU entirely: the overall organization would still be called Woman's Missionary Union, but everything else received a new name. WMS became Baptist Women for ladies over age 29. YWA became Baptist Young Women for young women ages 18-29; Acteens was a new group for junior high and high school girls, while Girls in Action was for girls in grades 1-6. Preschoolers who had been Sunbeams were now Mission Friends.

One transfer from WMU to Brotherhood was that of Royal Ambassadors (RAs) for young grade school boys. With the new groups came new magazines for most. Missouri WMU staff gained titles to match the new terminology: Mary Bidstrup remained Executive Secretary, but Nell Constantz became Baptist Women Director, Alberta Gilpin became Baptist Young Women Director, Beverly Goss became Acteens Director, and Adele Branson became Girls in Action/Mission Friends Director. These were drastic changes to accept, but the women of Missouri WMU worked to show their benefits while downplaying the negative aspect of modifying tradition.

The annual WMU Area Clinics were held with emphasis on training WMU women in the work before them in the new age level groups. State staff and volunteers were active in promoting a new program in any capacity possible. It was a busy time for Missouri WMU as it prepared for the new plan of organization, but traditional programs continued too.

Camp work received some focus when there was a special GA and RA Camp Directors Workshop held in 1970. There were also seven associational camp workshops. State camping continued, and GA camp was extended to seven weeks. The YWA Conference at Windermere was held, as was the YWA Convention and Intermediate GA Queens' Court. In addition, the Church Study Course was instituted so that WMU

CHAPTER 16

women could train for their work and receive some certification of this training.

Two new programs were introduced in 1971. The first was the 60 and Above Retreat held for senior citizens. This retreat, sponsored by WMU and the Brotherhood, became a favorite Windermere program. Later this retreat was renamed the Over 60 Retreat, and it was sponsored by the Family Ministries Department. The other new program was Teen Scene, the state Acteen convention. Junior high and high school girls from across the state gathered at Windermere during state teachers' meeting school break in the fall. Response was so overwhelming that the event had to be expanded in following years.

Another change for Missouri WMU was the move to a new Baptist Building in Jefferson City. Missouri Baptists had outgrown their facility on Adams Street, and a decision was made in 1964 to build a new Baptist Building. However, that decision was reversed in 1969 when the convention purchased the Missouri Motor Hotel Building. Following extensive remodeling, the WMU staff and other state workers moved into the new facilities at 400 East High Street in 1971.

Two of the program highlights for 1972 were missions conference for young adults. The Single Young Adults Missions Conference was held in March, and the Missions Conference for Married Young Adults was held later that year. Both of these conferences gave young women and men an opportunity to explore the world of missions as a future career. Another event was the Associational WMU Training Seminar, which was led by WMU staff.

Missouri Acteens were active in 1972 with several projects. A busload of Acteens journeyed to Glorieta in July for the first national Acteens Convention. Many of these same girls and numerous others attended Teen Scene at Windermere that November. Additionally, excitement spread among the girls when it was announced that the Executive Committee was considering awarding scholarships to girls based upon their achievement in Studiact. Studiact was the Acteens' achievement program which replaced Forward Steps in the 1970 WMU reorganization. Good things were happening to Missouri Acteens.

Giant Step was a program introduced by the national WMU in which Missouri WMU participated. The goals for the program were 25 increases in membership, the number of organizations, and magazine subscriptions. Trends were reversed nationally, and national WMU began to show gains instead of losses for the first time in ten years.

The Bidstrup era, which began with a series of celebrations, ended with a Missouri WMU celebration. At the 1973 Annual Meeting, Missouri WMU celebrated its 50th anniversary. A huge birthday party was held at Poplar Bluff, site of the first Missouri

CHAPTER 16

WMU meeting in 1923. Pageants, fashion shows, and historical vignettes were highlights of the festive occasion. Missouri WMU members were proud of their fifty years of WMU work.

Missouri WMU members were not as festive when Mary Bidstrup announced her retirement in June of 1973. Throughout the changes and adjustments for WMU work, Mary Bidstrup had remained a constant for Missouri WMU. For twenty-five years, Miss Bidstrup had loyally devoted her time and energy to the missions support cause in Missouri. She had seen missions support grow. Missouri WMU had a proud heritage, and Mary Bidstrup was a major contributor in its recent history. Following a gala farewell party, Miss Bidstrup left Jefferson City and the Baptist Building. However, she will never leave the hearts of the Missouri WMU women who knew and loved her. Mary O. Bidstrup passed away on December 17, 1990.

CHAPTER 17

The Leadership of Alberta Gilpin

Missouri WMU Executive Secretary
1973-2000

Alberta Gilpin assumed the position of Executive Secretary of the Missouri WMU in 1973 after Mary Bidstrup retired.

Alberta Jane Gilpin was born on March 11, 1942, in Columbia, to Wayne and Dorothy Gilpin. She spent her childhood near Ashland and accepted Christ at the age of 13 in August 1955 at Nashville Baptist Church in southern Boone County. Alberta was active in her local church. She was educated in Boone County schools. When Alberta began elementary school, a neighbor came by and took her to GAs. When she was

CHAPTER 17

15, Alberta felt God's call to some kind of church-related vocation.

After graduation from high school, she went to college at the University of Missouri, Columbia, where she earned a Bachelor of Science Degree in Speech Education. Still knowing that she felt God calling her to a church-related vocation, Alberta began the process of choosing a seminary. Alberta read about the mission opportunities for the students in the New Orleans Baptist Theological Seminary and felt this was the direction God was leading her. Alberta still remembers her first day in Helen Falls' seminary class on missions, and she felt God was opening the door to missions as a vocation. Alberta was appointed by the Home Mission Board as a student associate during her second year in seminary. She worked at The Good Samaritan Home, a rescue mission for women located in New Orleans while pursuing and obtaining a Master's Degree in Religious Education.

Near the end of her last year at the New Orleans Seminary, Alberta received a call from Mary Bidstrup, the WMU Executive Director of Missouri. She asked if Alberta would consider being interviewed for a position with Missouri WMU. Alberta said that she was not interested and thought she would apply for a position with the Home Mission Board. She was coming home for spring break, and Miss Bidstrup asked if she could stop by Jefferson City for a visit while she was home. Alberta first said, "No," but finally, she agreed to think about it. The Missouri WMU Annual Meeting was in session in Mexico, and Alberta met with the Personnel Committee there. She was surprised at how nice the ladies were, and she was troubled she had dismissed the possibility that working with the Missouri WMU might be God's plan for her life at this particular time.

Alberta was currently helping women rebuild their lives at the Good Samaritan Home. Here was an opportunity to work with other young women and help guide their lives, but should she? She sought direction from the Lord. After about a week, at 10:30 one night, the Lord directed her to go do WMU work in Missouri. Alberta called Miss Bidstrup, who had already received a telegram from the Personnel Committee saying the Lord had revealed to them that Alberta was the one for the job.

On June 1, 1967, Alberta began her professional association with WMU when she was hired as YWA/Sunbeam Band Director. Her title was changed to YWA Director in 1968 and then to BYW Director in 1970, and she served until 1973. From 1973-1993, Alberta was Woman's Missionary Union Director, then her title changed to Missions Education and Ministry Team Leader from 1993-1999. Another title change occurred when she became Missions Mobilization Initiative Coordinator 1999-2000. Even

CHAPTER 17

though Alberta had different job titles with the Missouri Baptist Convention, she was Missouri WMU's Executive Director.

When Alberta became Executive Secretary, Missouri WMU had a close relationship with the Missouri Baptist Convention. The women had proven that their work was important to the total program of Baptist work in Missouri. An office staff of five professional workers and two secretaries was devoted to carrying out the program drawn up by the Executive Committee. Viola Scherff was serving as President of the Missouri WMU, and she had the love and support of the women of the state. Missouri WMU had been through some hard times in terms of enrollment and support, but the women were optimistic that new programs handed down from national WMU would guide the organization into better times. The Missouri Woman's Missionary Union was a well-known and well-respected organization.

There were two positions open in the WMU department in 1973. The BYW director position had to be filled since Alberta Gilpin had advanced to Executive Secretary. One of the first staff members Alberta hired was a replacement for the BYW Director position. Alberta called Jan Currence, who had been very active in BYWs at Southwest Baptist College for four years. Jan's senior year, she was President of the on-campus BYWs with over 200 members. Jan comments: "I had just graduated from Southwest Baptist University when Alberta called me and asked if I would be interested in a job working with Baptist Young Women and College Young Women in Missouri. Alberta had confidence in me, and she reaffirmed my talents and abilities. As the WMU staff traveled all over the state, we shared stories of family, personal concerns, and just anything that came to mind. Alberta was easy to talk with, and she was a good listener." Jan Currence joined the WMU staff on September 1, 1973, as the Baptist Young Women's Director.

In the meantime, Beverly Goss had resigned to become Executive Director of WMU work in Arizona. Karen Panovich assumed the position of Acteens Director on September 12. Both of these new staff members were Missouri women who had experience in and were devoted to WMU work. They joined with Alberta Gilpin, Nell Constantz, and Adele Branson to create a new WMU staff to carry out the programs approved by the Executive Committee for the 53,901 members of Missouri WMU.

The work of Missouri WMU continued in 1974 with a few changes in programming and two major changes in personnel. One program change was the deletion of the *Missouri WMU News*. Now WMU members had to depend upon *Missouri WMU Facts and Features* and direct mailings for information. The

CHAPTER 17

first personnel change was the election of a new President since Mrs. Scherff had served her allowable term of five years.

In this history, I have tried to go in somewhat chronological order of events, but Alberta has such a long tenure with Missouri WMU, I'm not able to put all of the events related to her life in this one chapter about her. But I did want to include some major events that she said were important to her and also add some comments from past staff members and MWMU Presidents.

"Alberta was a leader, known not only in Missouri WMU but also in national WMU," recalls Jan Turner. "She served on many task force teams, for example, working on the national WMU dated plan. She was a respected leader not only on the WMU staff but also among the other staff members at the Baptist Building. Alberta was an organizer and an idea person. I have worked with Alberta on Policy and Procedures/Bylaw Committees and have seen her logical and organized approach in getting ideas across."

The following are some comments about Alberta from past WMU Presidents taken from the book *Enduring Love* written by Barbara Bray. "Her morning prayer life was, as far as I'm concerned, is what set Alberta apart as a Christian and a visionary leader," writes Dawn Phillips, a past WMU President.

"She simply didn't talk about prayer to us; she truly listened to the Father in prayer. I believe her perseverance, her popularity, her friendship, her faith, her generosity, her ethnicity, and her success were a direct result of her commitment to hearing from God before anyone else each day."

Dawn Phillips said, "Speaking of Alberta's vision, I never ceased to be stunned by her 'crazy' ideas that, when we followed through with them, they proved to be God's gift. For example, her idea to add a prayer coordinator to the Missouri WMU Executive Committee was a lovely idea in and of itself. Before many months had passed, we realized why God had given her the concept when Randy Sprinkle came to her with his God-given revelation for what became our special prayer emphasis named Lift Up Lesotho."

Barbara Bray remembers when we started *PrayerWays* and Marilyn Coble, our first Prayer Coordinator, had a prayer request for Lesotho as well as for all Missouri missionaries on their birthday. Satan had firm control over that small African nation in South Africa, and he fought us on every hand, but Missouri Baptist Women prayed. Today, we still pray for Lesotho, plus we also pray for other missionaries, pastors, and churches. Missouri WMU continues to have a board member who composes the *Prayer-Ways*.

Norma Altis, past MWMU President, writes about this experience. "Randy and Nancy Sprinkle, Marilyn Coble, Prayer Coordinator, Alberta, and I met in Jefferson City at the Baptist Building just a few days before Christmas in 1986. Alberta knew it was surely of the Lord when we could all meet on this day. We all wanted to accept Randy's challenge to 'Lift Up Lesotho' and came up with an action plan to get Missouri women involved. It was such a joy to ride and share together as we covered the state that week. Randy told us funny stories from the mission field. I do remember how much we laughed, especially Alberta. Everywhere we went, the reaction of the women around the state was positive, and they had great ideas on how to promote the partnership. Alberta said that she was so blessed and appreciated the response of Missouri women. It was more than she expected."

When Barbara Bray was elected President of Missouri WMU in 1981, Missouri churches were entering into a partnership with the Taiwan Baptist Convention. Barbara and her husband Tom had been asked to go with a group of pastors to visit Taiwan and hold revivals. One day Alberta called Barbara and asked if she had a passport. Alberta told Barbara of her vision to have a prayer link up with the WMU women of Taiwan. Alberta wanted Barbara to accompany herself and Marilyn Coble, Prayer

Coordinator for Missouri WMU. They would be going to Taiwan to meet with the Taiwan WMU Executive Board and attend their WMU Annual Meeting in November.

Norma Altis remembers the excitement of attending the Centennial Celebration of the national WMU in Richmond, Virginia, in 1988. Missouri took seven busloads of women to attend. Alberta, Laura Mason, and Norma (MWMU President in 1988) were privileged to ride in a vintage convertible representing Missouri WMU in the parade of the states. Dressed in her Centennial dress with a wide-brimmed hat and waving to the crowd of over 10,000 attendees, Alberta thoroughly enjoyed being in the parade.

Barbara Bray said, "The real highlight of the trip occurred on the way home when one bus challenged the others to give to the Lottie Moon Christmas Offering as the goal had not been reached. Some women gave all they had, and a big offering was collected. Alberta was overwhelmed at the response and also concerned because some had truly given all they had. These women had sacrificed a lot just to make the trip. They were truly mission-minded. Alberta was a great leader who showed us the way to do missions as she lived it out in her life each day. Alberta Gilpin was a godly woman, a woman of prayer, always a true friend, a mentor, and a generous person who had a mission heart."

Barbara Bray also said she was able to observe on many occasions that wherever they went, "Alberta was always able to recall the name of each woman she had met across the state. She made each individual feel special. She never appeared hurried and listened to each one with the same attentiveness regardless of position or influence."

When Barbara Bray became WMU President, she marveled at Alberta's organizational skills. Barbara said, "I will never forget when she opened a drawer and showed me her system of preparing for events. For every month, she had made a list of what needed to be done." Alberta remarked, "If something happens to me, here is all that you will need to keep these events on target."

According to Dawn Phillips, past MWMU President, another of Alberta's visions was the partnership of Missouri Baptists with Belarus. "I'll never forget the morning Alberta had been praying and said, 'This may be the craziest thing I've ever said to you, but what if we gave the Belarusian women our Annual Meeting?'" The rest is history. Our 1995 meeting with the women in Belarus helped them gain momentum to organize and become a part of the Women's Department of Baptist World Alliance and to begin truly to function in Baptist life in Belarus. A new day had come to them. God had entrusted His idea to Alberta, and she was faithful."

Norma Altis said, "Alberta gave some of us opportunities we would never have envisioned. The women's meeting in Belarus was one of those. She and the staff planned so many things for us. All women were included whether you actually made the trip or stayed in Missouri and prayed and took over the responsibilities of the women who could go. Gifts were collected from women and girls to take to the Belarusian women. Everyone could be involved and feel a part of the ministry."

Norma Altis, past President of Missouri WMU, also remembers Alberta's relating well to both men and women who dearly loved and respected her. She was a true friend to her peers at the Baptist Building. "She hurt when they hurt and rejoiced with them when they rejoiced. They were also there for her, especially when she sponsored her Romanian family and offered help with each challenge."

Many WMU women who made this trip regard it as a life-changing experience. Barbara Popp, former MWMU President, shares: "I had the privilege of being invited to a small group meeting in the early part of 1994. At this meeting, Alberta shared with us how God was leading her to realize Missouri WMU needed to become involved with the women of Belarus. At this point, I had read about the partnership between Missouri Baptists and Belarusian Christians, and I had been curious about

CHAPTER 17

all the plans between the two groups. As she shared her vision about Missouri WMU members traveling to Belarus and hosting a Woman's Meeting in Minsk, I listened but had many questions about the blueprint placed before us. I had worked closely with Alberta and trusted her judgment because I had learned she really prayed before any and every plan was made! Both of these trips to Belarus blessed me beyond description! They changed my heart and life...they were unforgettable, touching, heart-piercing experiences. If we were told once, we heard dozens of times from both men and women—our sisters and brothers in Christ—what Missouri women coming meant, what a confirmation of a vision from God given to a godly woman like Alberta!"

For Debbie Miller serving on the WMU staff with Alberta for over 17 years was a time of learning and growing. "Alberta was a true mentor to me; she always confirmed and encouraged me. Alberta was a 'big picture' person. She loved planning for the future, and her insight and her desire to try new things challenged me."

Debbie Miller writes that one of her greatest treasures was having Alberta as a friend. "She probably knows me as well as anybody does. It is to her that I have turned in good times and bad. I have shared joys and sorrows with her. She is a wonderful counselor, never telling me what to do but always offering sound suggestions. She is a friend who believes in me, and I know she has made me a better person."

Geri Williams, secretary in the WMU Department, said, "I learned more about leadership from watching Alberta than from any book. She was such an encourager. She always encouraged me to do things I never thought I'd be able to do. She gave us a feeling of ownership in what we were doing in the WMU Department."

Lorene Murphy, former state WMU President states: "When Alberta was called to work in Jefferson City for Missouri WMU, I was pleased. We needed her in a great way, and she had so much to give. As an associational president (now called director) attending the meetings in the Baptist Building in Jefferson City, I learned a great deal from Alberta. She always seemed so poised, quite knowledgeable about WMU, and willing to listen as we worked together to improve Missouri WMU. Alberta was a wonderful teacher. I learned a great deal from watching her, listening to her, and working with her. She was always ready and willing to offer help and good ideas to keep me on track."

Lorene also appreciated Alberta's ability to be humorous to get us to relax and laugh. "There were times in long-range planning sessions when we seemed to lose our focus. Then she could lead us back into planning, and the ideas would flow. There were many times when we were really trying to put things together, and they just seemed not to go together. Then something funny would happen, and that laughter would cause us all to laugh with her. Alberta had a contagious laugh!"

Others outside of Missouri Baptist circles also recognized Alberta's leadership skills, as evident in the recognitions she received. In 1989, William Jewell College named her a Walter Pope Binns Fellow in recognition and appreciation for service and ministry. In 2000, she was listed in the *International Who's Who of Women Executives*. She was also named to the list of Outstanding Young Women of America in 1970. She received the Outstanding Religious Educator Award in 2000.

The following resolution was presented to Alberta, following her resignation, at the April 20-21, 2001, WMU Annual Meeting at South Haven Baptist Church in Springfield.

Resolution of the Executive Board of the Missouri Baptist Convention

- *Whereas, Alberta Gilpin served Missouri Baptists faithfully for many years as Woman's Missionary Union Executive Director and as a member of the Executive Board Staff; and*
- *Whereas, Alberta Gilpin was instrumental in*

the purchasing, furnishing, and ongoing program of the Missionary-In-Residence House located at 1507 Vieth Drive, Jefferson City;

- *Be It Resolved, that the Missionary-In-Residence House located at 1507 Vieth Drive, Jefferson City, be officially known as the "Gilpin Missionary House" in honor of Alberta Gilpin; and*
- *Be It Finally Resolved, that this resolution be presented to Alberta Gilpin at the Missouri Woman's Missionary Union Annual Meeting in Springfield, Missouri, April 20, 2001.*
- *Adopted by the Executive Board of the Missouri Baptist Convention in session April 10, 2001.*

Another resolution was given to Alberta from the Missouri WMU board on April 20, 2001.

Resolution in honor of Alberta Gilpin

- *Whereas, Missouri Woman's Missionary Union has been blessed for 33 years through the ministry and leadership of Alberta Gilpin; and*
- *Whereas, Alberta Gilpin has modeled for Missouri Baptists the WMU Watchword "Laborers together with God" (1 Corinthians 3:9; and*
- *Whereas, Alberta Gilpin has retired from the Missouri Baptist Convention in December*

2000; and

- *Whereas, Alberta has served as YWA Director from 1967-1970, as BYW Director from 1970-1973, as WMU Executive Secretary from 1973-1975 and as Missouri WMU Director from 1975-2000; and*
- *Whereas, Alberta has also served Missouri Baptist Convention as Mission Education and Ministry Development Team Leader and as Missions Mobilization Coordinator; and*
- *Whereas, under Alberta's leadership Missouri began the first prayer partnership network with Lesotho and linked partnership with women in Taiwan and Belarus; and*
- *Whereas, under Alberta's leadership she has helped strengthen the missions vision through Missouri Woman's Missionary Union; and*
- *Whereas, Alberta has exhibited a ministry lifestyle that extended beyond her professional life into her personal life is demonstrated by adopting the Raffa family in April 1986, who were refugees from Romania.*

Therefore, be it resolved, that we the members of Woman's Missionary Union attending the 77th Missouri WMU Annual Meeting held April 20-21, 2001 at South Haven Baptist Church in Springfield, Missouri express our appreciation and gratitude for the thirty-three years of faithful and dedicated service to the Lord through Missouri WMU and the

Missouri Baptist Convention by naming Alberta Gilpin, Missouri WMU Director Emeritus.

Therefore, be it resolved, that the newly established WMU Operating Fund be designated as the Missouri WMU Alberta Gilpin Fund to be used for special Missouri WMU Projects and other uses as approved by the MWMU Board. It is with great pleasure to announce that as of April 19, 2001, there has been over $8,700.00 received in honor of Alberta Gilpin.

Therefore, be it further resolved, that this resolution be presented to Alberta Gilpin on April 20, 2001 with all the love and appreciation it can hold from the more than 28,000 members of Missouri Woman's Missionary Union.

Debbie Miller	*Kathy Scott*	*Jan Turner*
MWMU President	*WMU Executive Director*	*Communications Consultant*

During the years working with the Missouri Baptist Convention, Alberta had always lived in several types of homes. She had lived in apartments and condos but always missed living in a place where she could settle in and feel that she was at home. She bought a home, but owning a home made her feel guilty since she spent so much time traveling. She asked herself if she wanted to share her privacy with someone else. She did want to share her home, so she invited a refugee couple, Tudor and Maria Rafa, to live with her after they escaped from Communist Romania in April 1986.

CHAPTER 17

She took this refugee couple into her home and heart, and thus they became part of the WMU family. Alberta not only taught about missions, but she lived a missions lifestyle. The joy of loving this young couple was hampered, though, because they had left behind many family members, including their son and daughter in Romania. Prayers went up from Missouri WMU that God would guide Alberta, Tudor, and Maria as they began their new adventure and dreamed of bringing the Rafa's children, Calin and Ramona, to Missouri also.

Carla Stegeman, secretary in the WMU Department, remembers when Alberta was considering sponsoring a refugee family. "She was a single woman with a new house and a stable income. She decided she needed to share the blessings God had given her with others."

Maria, after their arrival in Missouri, told Alberta that before they came to the United States, people had questioned her and Tudor. "Aren't you afraid to go live with a total stranger? What if this person abuses you or makes you a servant? What if she doesn't feed you or take care of you? What if she lets you down?" Alberta asked her, "What did you reply?" Maria said, "I told them we had prayed, and we thought this was what we were supposed to do."

Alberta then told Maria that people had questioned her similarly. "What if these refugees hurt you? Tear up your stuff? What if they are mean and dirty and violent and abusive and lazy?"

"What did you tell them?" Maria questioned.

Alberta replied, "That I prayed, and I thought this is what God wanted me to do. I trusted Him."

The journey from Romania to Jefferson City, Missouri, was not an easy one for the Rafas. In 2006 on President's Day, Barbara Bray met with Alberta, Tudor, and Maria. She wanted them to tell the story from their point of view. Tudor was working as an electrician in a power plant in Romania. He was 25 years old and wanted to further his career, so he sought a more responsible position with the company, only to be told that to have a better position, he must join the Communist Party. So, he thought, "Well, I will join the Communist Party." There were special interviews and procedures to follow. One time in speaking to a party member Tudor commented, "People like you are ruining our country." That sealed his fate and any chance for a promotion.

By 1984, Tudor felt that in order to make a future for his family, he had to leave Romania. Tudor and his wife began planning to leave the country together, leaving their two children, who were 4 and 6 years old, behind. They were too young to make such a difficult journey. Maria's sister and brother-in-law moved into the Rafas' apartment, so the Rafas could avoid suspicion. One night Maria and Tudor began their difficult journey. When Maria did not show up for work, the authorities knew something was wrong, for she had never missed a day of work before. They were able to arrive in Yugoslavia and make it across the border into Italy and to safety.

When Tudor and Maria got off the airplane in Columbia, Alberta was there to meet them. Alberta had arranged for a Jefferson City man who spoke Romanian to meet the plane with her. The Rafas spoke little English, and Alberta spoke no Romanian. Many funny and frustrating experiences happened along the way as they learned to communicate.

The children remained with other family members in Romania. Alberta worked with government agencies, senators, the American Red Cross, and anyone else who could help them to get clearance for the children to come to the United States. This was a difficult challenge! Women all over the state were praying for this to be accomplished. After 18 long months, the children arrived in New York City on July 1987. Alberta was there to bring them back to her home. Calin was eight years old, and Ramona was six years old.

"Maria and Tudor truly became her children in a short time," Norma Altis writes. "Many telephone calls came from Tudor or Maria when I traveled with Alberta while I was President. She was always patient with them in her explanations. One time they told her they had gotten a doll and put it on her bed to remind them of her when she was away because they missed her so much. With the downfall of communism, other friends and family have come from Romania, and Alberta has taught at least ten of them to drive."

Alberta always says what a blessing this family has been in her life, and the Rafa family adores her. Tudor told Barbara Bray, "We owe everything to Alberta, and we will always take care of her when she needs us."

Alberta loves and appreciates Tudor and Maria. She said, "The Rafas have brought a dimension to my life that I would never have gained through all the mission studies or reading of mission books. I have learned about another culture firsthand. I lived through the fall of communism. Through their eyes and ears, I learned what freedom really is. I had never appreciated my freedom until I met them. I learned what sacrifice really means. They have taught me much about accepting people like they are and not trying to change them to be what you want them to be. I now have two children, four grandchildren, and two great-grandchildren. How blessed I am! You can never outgive God."

CHAPTER 18

The Presidency of Marilyn Harris Coble

Missouri WMU President
1974-1976

At the March 28-30, 1974 Annual Meeting held at Windermere Baptist Assembly, Mrs. Marilyn Coble was chosen as the new Missouri WMU President. One of her first duties was to regretfully accept the resignation of Mrs. Nell Constantz. Nell had devotedly served Missouri WMU for twenty years as Baptist Women Director but decided that she should retire. As with any woman who has WMU in her heart, Mrs. Constantz left the Missouri WMU office, but missions continued to be a top priority after her retirement. Budget cutbacks prevented the WMU Department from filling Mrs. Constantz's position, so Mrs. Coble led Missouri Baptist Women with the aid of Gilpin,

Currence, Panovich, and Branson.

Marilyn Jean Harris was born August 23, 1924, in Fort Scott, Kansas, to Ernest and Gladine Harris. She attended Ft. Scott public schools and Ft. Scott Junior College. Marilyn accepted Christ at age seven and joined the First Baptist Church in Ft. Scott. On April 28, 1944, she married Fred O. Coble in Norfolk, Virginia. Two daughters and two sons joined the family over the years, and Marilyn kept busy being a wife, mother, and active church member. WMU work was an important part of her life, and she worked with Mission Friends, Girls in Action, and WMU in her church and association. Special interests of Marilyn's were in the areas of prayer support and work with National Baptists. Marilyn served as an area member of the WMU Executive Committee prior to her election as state President in 1974. Marilyn served as state President and national WMU Vice-President from Missouri until 1976. Later Marilyn was instrumental in the addition of a WMU Prayer Coordinator to the list of state officers. She became the first Prayer Coordinator in 1983 and served for five years. Marilyn helped start *PrayerWays.*

Traditional programming continued in 1974 under the leadership of Mrs. Coble. The Baptist Woman's Missionary Council, Madge N. Truex Fund programs, bus trip to Glorieta, Over 60 Retreat, WMU Week at Windermere, Area WMU Clinics, and Camp

Windermere for Girls were a few of the longstanding programs.

Teen Scene kept growing, and in 1974, it was split so that there was a session for girls from both the east and west sides of the state. Another Acteens program, which began in 1974, was the establishment of Acteen scholarships. These scholarships were available to young women in the state who had reached high levels of achievement in Studiact. Funds were provided by the four Baptist colleges in Missouri, so recipients had to apply for this funding through one of these institutions. Because of the support given by these schools, hundreds of Acteens received some financial assistance due to this program.

A new Girls in Action program for 1974 was a series of five GA Caravans. Instead of attempting to bring all GA's together for a convention, the caravans took the Girls in Action program to regional gatherings. The one-day meetings held in the spring were a success and continued through 1978.

By 1975, the Missouri Baptist Convention had a new Executive Director. Dr. Rheubin South came to Missouri from an Arkansas pastorate. Under his leadership, the convention was able to unite to provide an efficient, mission-minded cooperative body. His directorship had an impact on WMU, as did that of his predecessors. The MBC had to tighten its purse strings following the death of Earl Harding. One result of this was the elimination of the Baptist Women's Director position in the WMU Department. Funding grew even tighter in December 1975 when the position of Sunbeam director was eliminated following the retirement of Mrs. Adele Branson. Additionally, the MBC changed the name of the WMU Executive Secretary position. Since other MBC department heads were called "Directors," the head of the WMU department became the WMU Director. Another name change, which came about in 1975, affected Karen Panovich, who married Tim Helzer while still serving as Acteens Director, so she became Karen Helzer.

There were some new administrative changes, which had an origin at the national WMU. The four tasks of WMU were reworded in October 1975. The new tasks added direct evangelism to mission study, mission support, and mission action. There was also a new report system which became effective at the start of the WMU year on October 1.

The first action of the Missouri WMU Executive Committee for 1976 was the hiring of a new Acteens Director since Karen Helzer had resigned late in 1975. Donna Maples, who had been a state camp worker for several summers, was hired as the Acteens Director in January of 1976. Jan Currence was given the title of Baptist Women and Baptist Young Women Director in 1976.

CHAPTER 18

With the coming of spring, there was another vacancy to fill since Mrs. Marilyn Coble had resigned her presidency in 1976 because she and her husband were moving to Sterling, Illinois. Marilyn had served on the Missouri WMU Executive Board for 16 years. She assisted in the establishment of the national Baptist and Southern Baptist Women's Missionary Fellowship Interracial Council. She was instrumental in the establishment of the Lesotho and Missouri Prayer Partnership. Her family said this about her in her obituary, "Her true passion was directed within the Woman's Missionary Union." Marilyn Coble went to her heavenly home on November 8, 2020, at the age of 96.

CHAPTER 19
The Presidency of Lorene Hamblen Murphy

Missouri WMU President
1976-1981

The next WMU President was Mrs. Lorene Murphy of Kansas City. Lorene Ruth Hamblen was born in North Kansas City on November 25, 1926. Her parents were John and Anna Hamblen. Her childhood was filled with church activities since her father was a pastor. She accepted Christ on Easter Sunday morning in 1935. She lived in North Kansas City her entire childhood and graduated from North Kansas City high school. On March 24, 1946, she married Donald Leslie Murphy, and later the family grew with the birth of a son and daughter. Mrs. Murphy was active in her local church and associational WMU.

CHAPTER 19

She became an area member of the Missouri WMU Executive Committee in 1970 and served as recording secretary from 1974-1975. She was elected state President in 1976 and served until 1981.

The primary yearly publication of the Missouri WMU received a new name in 1976. *Missouri WMU Facts and Features* became *Missouri Woman's Missionary Union Resource Book*. The expanded handbook included directories of staff and officers, By-Laws, Annual Meeting Minutes, Book of Reports, General Missouri WMU Information, Missouri Missionary Information, and a listing of approved workers. A new facet of Missouri WMU which was introduced in 1976, was the role of approved workers. Since the state professional staff had been cut back to three, the women of Missouri WMU volunteered to take over some of the workload previously carried by the staff of five. One way that this was done was through Special Workers, who were ladies trained to teach conferences on the various WMU age level groups. Once a woman was trained and certified, she could teach about WMU, Baptist Women, Baptist Young Women, Acteens, Girls in Action, or Mission Friends.

Area Meetings were held for the last time in October of 1976. These meetings were useful and popular, but a more cost-effective means of training women was needed. Other programs continued to prosper, among them Camp Directors' Workshop, Baptist Woman's Missionary Council Meetings, Annual Meeting, GA Missions Caravans, Camp Windermere for Girls, WMU Conference, Over 60 Retreat, and Teen Scene. A new program for 1976 was a series of Area BYW Get-Togethers.

One staff change occurred in March 1977, when Jan Currence resigned her position to marry Rev. Phil Turner, a pastor from Marshall, Missouri. She was replaced by Carrol Kelly, who assumed the work of Baptist Women and Baptist Young Women. Carrol joined Alberta Gilpin, who served as WMU director, and Donna Maples, who devoted her time to Acteens and Girls in Action.

A new program for 1977 was a set of Regional Leadership Training Conferences. These six meetings, held in key locations across the state, served as a replacement for the twenty-four Area Clinics which had been held in the past.

The 1978 Annual Meeting was one in which Missouri WMU women once again revised their Bylaws. It was a trying time for President Lorene Murphy since she fell off the platform at the beginning of the meeting. Though she had to preside from the front pew with her foot propped up on a chair, her leadership was effective. Missouri WMU women accepted the new Bylaws. The main changes were the expansion of the number of members-at-large from

CHAPTER 19

ten to twenty on the Executive Committee, the Vice-President, became chairman of the Truex Fund budget committee, and changing the titles of professional staff.

In 1978, the Missouri WMU endorsed the SBC Bold Mission Thrust program and became whole-hearted supporters of this evangelistic effort. In the following years, many Missouri WMU members were able to participate in this program, especially through the MBC Bold Mission Taiwan program.

Another personnel change came about in 1978 when Carrol Kelly left Missouri WMU to become a Baptist Women Consultant for national WMU in Birmingham. Debbie Bailey from St. Louis became the new Baptist Women and Baptist Young Women Director for Missouri. One last change for 1978 was the expansion of communication about WMU programming. The first issue of *The Outlook* was published in October of that year. This streamlined quarterly newsletter gave information of upcoming activities and provided local and associational leaders with registration forms and clipart to be used in promoting those activities. Another means of communication was the inclusion of a WMU promotional page in the *Word and Way*.

The fact that Missouri was the SBC leader in WMU leadership diplomas through the Church Study Course program brought positive publicity to

Missouri WMU in 1978. Missouri continued its tradition of being a WMU dedicated to study and training.

The Executive Committee of Missouri WMU did not remain static. During 1979, the Executive Board of the MBC approved a restructuring of the WMU Department; the restructuring had its origin in the Missouri WMU itself. Since the WMU Department didn't have enough staff to provide a worker for each of the age level groups, the women suggested that a new structure might be more beneficial. After much consideration, the WMU Executive Committee recommended that there be three positions within the WMU Department beginning on January 1, 1980, with the workload divided as follows: Alberta Gilpin (WMU Director) in charge of the overall program but also devoting attention to associational WMU work; Donna Maples (Associate) in charge of development of new organizations; and Debbie Bailey (Associate) in charge of skills training. This structure met with success in Missouri, and it has been emulated in other state WMUs because of its innovative nature and its applicability to WMU work.

While the WMU office was getting accustomed to the new structure, the Missouri WMU program continued to flourish. During 1980 there were bus tours to Glorieta, five weeks of Camp Windermere for Girls, three Over 60 Retreats, the first high school

CHAPTER 19

Acteens Retreat, meetings of the Baptist Woman's Missionary Council, a BYW Retreat, a Mission Friends Institute, Camp Directors' Workshop, and additional training events. In 1980, there were 49,052 members of WMU with numerous opportunities for training.

Enlistment of new members was a special focus of national WMU in the 1980s. Something had to be done to counter the downswing in membership across the SBC, so several new programs were implemented. One new national WMU program which began in 1980 was Starteam. Missouri participated in this three-year-enlistment campaign, which had as its main goal the creation of new local WMUs. A team of ten women who were specially trained for the task worked throughout the state to encourage churches to create WMUs. Through cooperation with Directors of Missions, pastors, and associational WMU directors, the Missouri Starteam produced increased enlistment at first. The three-year program was concluded in 1985.

The Show Me 3800 enrollment campaign was another enlistment program completed in 1980. Missouri WMU met and exceeded the goal. Over 4,200 women and children were enlisted for WMU work at the local level. It was hoped that this would indicate an upswing in membership trends.

While much attention was given to new members and new WMUs in 1980, the Madge N. Truex Fund was continuing as one of the best programs of Missouri WMU. Part of the reason for the success of the Truex Fund has been its flexibility over the years to adapt with the times. Two changes were made in 1980, which helped keep the Truex Fund up-to-date. The first change was the inclusion of missionary associate in the definition of a Missouri missionary. This Foreign Mission Board position had become popular among Baptists, so Missouri WMU enlarged its definition to enable associates to reap the benefits of the Truex Fund. The second change had to deal with the scholarship rules. The Executive Committee decided to alter the Truex Fund so that students attending graduate school rather than seminary would also be eligible for funds. This allowed assistance for those who wished to go into full-time Christian service but were unable to attend a seminary in order to get the training of their choice. The changes were acceptable to Missouri WMU since local groups continued to faithfully support the fund with their contributions.

Donna Maples resigned the Missouri WMU staff at the end of 1980 to pursue a doctorate degree at the University of Missouri. By February 1, 1981, Lera Turner had been hired to fill the associate position dealing with new organizations. Missouri WMU continued to stress enlistment throughout 1981.

CHAPTER 19

Two other personnel changes came about at the WMU Annual Meeting in April 1981. Lorene Murphy stepped down as WMU President because she had served the maximum five-year term. Mrs. Barbara Bray was nominated as the new President and elected by those at the meeting. Also, the position of WMU Historian was added to the officers. Earlene Rogers of Higginsville was elected to this reactivated position, and she set about to preserve Missouri WMU's history.

Lorene Murphy went to her heavenly home on September 11, 2015, at the age of 88 years old.

CHAPTER 20

The Presidency of Barbara Birt Bray

Missouri WMU President
1981-1986

Barbara Joan Birt was born on May 17, 1931, in Hutchinson, Kansas, to Ken and Harriette Birt. She accepted Christ at age fourteen at the First Baptist Church in Joplin and began a life of Christian service. Barbara attended public schools and later received her Bachelor of Arts degree in 1952 from Blue Mountain College in Mississippi. On June 2, 1953, she married Rev. Tom Bray and began the active life of a pastor's wife. As the couple served churches throughout the Southland, Mrs. Bray devoted her time to her growing family of five children and remained active in her church work, especially WMU. Barbara worked primarily with Baptist Women and the general administration of WMU. She served on the Arkansas WMU Executive Committee from 1967-1970. Barbara served on the Missouri WMU Executive Committee from 1973-1976 and 1980-1981. She served on the Kentucky WMU Executive Board from 1976-1979. Barbara Bray was elected President of Missouri WMU in 1981 and served in that position until 1986.

Mrs. Bray led the Missouri WMU through 1981 as it continued traditional programs and strengthened new ones. The traditional programs continued in popularity with WMU members. New programs such as Starteam and a WMUniversity received special attention, and the women were proud to see that the new ideas were reaping new results.

Another change in 1982, which affected Acteens and Girls in Action, was the hiring of a camp director. In the past, one of the professional staff had assumed this responsibility, but in 1982 the WMU staff decided to hire a young woman to handle the camp program. Nancy Campbell was the first camp director, and she was succeeded by Becky Castleberry in 1984.

A Children's Mission Carnival brought 315 children into the Annual Meeting in 1982 and gave the children contact with missionaries and missions. Another new program was seven Leadership Training Events. At these meetings, state workers were invited by associations to train local WMU leaders. The concept met with success.

One of the highlights of the year for President Bray was the opportunity to participate in Bold Mission Taiwan. The MWMU Executive Committee allocated Truex Fund monies so that the WMU President could represent Missouri WMU in the activities in Taiwan, including the Taiwan WMU Annual Meeting. Alberta Gilpin and Debbie Bailey participated in Bold Mission Taiwan in 1981 and 1982, respectively. In addition, many Missouri WMU women provided their own financing and journeyed to Taiwan to participate in these life-changing experiences.

A new program, which was in the developmental stages in 1982, was a statewide prayer network. The Missouri WMU was one of three states involved in a national WMU pilot program to establish a system of in-depth prayer support for missionaries. The Missouri network plan, which was approved in November 1982, began with a state prayer coordinator who is responsible for compiling a list of prayer requests from missionaries. This list is sent to associational prayer coordinators, who then share the information with local WMU organizations through church prayer coordinators. The monthly *Missouri Missions Prayer Request* contained personal requests from Missouri missionaries, prayer requests for SBC and MBC meetings, missions crisis situations, Iowa WMU requests, Taiwan WMU requests, prayer for missionaries to be "called out," information about

Missouri Foreign and North American mission volunteers, and requests for volunteers. This prayer network is distinctive to Missouri and has been a blessing to all involved in it.

There were several changes in the Missouri WMU organization in 1983. The state prayer coordinator was added to the list of officers, and the Missouri Acteens council members were made *ex officio* Executive Committee members so that they could provide input into the sessions and also learn about the working of Missouri WMU. Finally, one woman was nominated and elected from each of the 12 areas to serve as area representatives on the Executive Committee. It was hoped that these changes would improve communication between the WMU Executive Committee and the women in the state.

Contributions to the Madge N. Truex Fund continued to be strong in 1983, so some additional scholarships were granted, as well as some special funding. A gift of $1,000 was sent to the Iowa Southern Baptist Fellowship in the beginning of 1983 to help support an interim WMU director. Also, $1,000 was sent to help pay for the new WMU building in Birmingham, Alabama. Missouri WMU attempted to be a faithful steward of the monies given to it, and these programs show that financial gifts were one aspect of that stewardship.

The Missouri WMU was saddened when they accepted the resignation of associate Lera Turner. However, this was countered by the joy of knowing that Lera was resigning in order to marry another Baptist Building employee, John Hardin. The associate position was filled by Donna McCollum on January 1, 1984. Soon the new staff of Gilpin, Bailey, and McCollum were busy carrying out the plans of the Executive Committee. The Missouri Baptist Convention was having its sesquicentennial in 1984, and Missouri WMU had a full slate of activities that demonstrated that missions support was still a major priority in the lives of Missouri Baptist Women.

The Bylaws of the Missouri WMU were revised in 1984 to change the basic governance of the organization. Up until that time, the Executive Committee had consisted of a large group of women from the state. This proved to be unmanageable; therefore, the Bylaws were altered so that there would be an Executive Committee made up of the elected officers and the area members. A new officer, Public Relations Coordinator, was added to the Executive Committee. Mrs. Polly Hosler from Carrollton was elected to fill this position. The Executive Committee remained as the main governing group. The Missouri WMU Council, which was composed of the Executive Committee, Past Presidents and Past WMU Executive Directors, and all associational WMU directors was created. This body provides valuable input to the Executive Committee and conveys information from the Executive Committee back to the association and local organizations.

Camp Windermere for Girls celebrated its twenty-fifth anniversary in 1984. Those who participated in the state camping program during its existence realized its value to their lives and celebrated the anniversary throughout the summer. There were four weeks of GA camp at Windermere in 1984. Acteens were urged to attend the national Acteens Convention (NAC) in Fort Worth, Texas. Missouri took four busloads of Acteen girls to Texas.

Missouri WMU was proud to host the national WMU Annual Meeting in Kansas City in June 1984. This added another event to their busy calendar, but the opportunities afforded by having a WMU national Annual Meeting in the state far outweighed the discomfort of an increased workload.

In the summer of 1984, Donna Maples became Training Design Group manager with national WMU. She joined Bobbie Sorrill and Carrol Kelly as former Missouri WMU staffers who went on to become members of the national staff. Maples and Kelley served at national WMU in Birmingham until December 1985 when both accepted positions with Tennessee WMU.

The Missouri WMU Council voted in October 1984 to support the fundraising efforts for the new national WMU building in Birmingham by pledging $17,000 for a Missouri Room. Many of the state WMUs which were part of the formation of national WMU in 1888 had funded and furnished rooms that now bear their names. The WMU Council wished to establish a Missouri Room, so a campaign was started by the Associational WMU directors to allow local WMU members to contribute. Today Missouri women can visit the building on New Hope Mountain in Birmingham and take pride in their part in it because of their gifts toward the Middle East Conference Room sponsored by Missouri WMU.

In 1988, Missouri WMU was asked to help furnish the Middle East Conference Room. The conference room has a long conference-type table that came from the old WMU headquarters and seated about 16 people. National WMU was in need of a piece of furniture for this room that would provide a place to serve food and store supplies. Alberta Gilpin appointed a committee of three from the WMU Board to develop this idea. Jan Currence Turner, Public Relations Director at the time, was chairman of the committee. Also serving on the committee were Millie Groves and Eleanor Speaker.

Jan had a friend and deacon in her church, First Baptist of Monroe City, Dennis Carson, who was a furniture/cabinet maker. Jan worked with Catherine Allen, on the national WMU staff, in designing the piece of furniture. Jan and Dennis designed a buffet/credenza that would be eight feet in length, about two feet in depth, and about three feet in height. It would have shelves on each side, drawers, enclosed cabinet doors, and would have a door in the middle with shelves for storage. A stained-glass insert with a Missouri state outline would be in the middle door, and in the center of the state would be an outline of the WMU emblem. There was also a light installed behind the stained glass. The stained glass was made in Springfield, Missouri. The credenza was made of native Missouri walnut wood and was treated with five coats of finish.

In order to pay for this credenza, MWMU asked the Associational WMU Directors to give a gift of $15.00 or more to help fund this project. There were 54 associations that participated in giving, and some individuals gave toward the project for a total of $1,725. Once the credenza was completed, Eleanor

Speaker and her husband loaded it in their van and delivered it to Birmingham.

National WMU recognized that its centennial was fast approaching, so plans were started in the early 1980s to prepare for a big celebration in 1987-1988. Missouri joined in the pre-celebration activities as early as 1981 when a historian was added to the officers of the organization. Earlene Rogers of Higginsville was elected as the first historian. An enlistment campaign known as Mission Vision 88 was instituted by the national WMU. Missouri joined the campaign and extended it to be known as Mission Vision 90. In the fall of 1984, Laura Mason was selected to write the state WMU history and to train associational and local WMU history writers. All associations and churches were urged to find someone to write their WMU histories in 1984-1985. Associational history writers were trained in January of 1985, and local writers received information from them, Mrs. Mason, the state WMU office, and the national WMU office.

While this pre-centennial work was going on, Missouri WMU continued to have statewide programs and projects. The traditional programs of Camp Director/Staff Workshop, WMU Annual Meeting, Camp Windermere for Girls, WMU Bus Trip to Ridgecrest, WMU Conference, Teen Scene, Missionary Families Retreat, and Career Missions

CHAPTER 20

Volunteer Workshop were held. A new program in 1985 was a statewide GA Retreat held at Windermere. Response was so great that some GAs had to be housed in hotels in nearby Camdenton because Windermere facilities were filled to capacity.

In December 1985, Donna McCollum resigned her associate position to marry Tom Albinson. Donna was succeeded by Kathy Stahr, who had been doing church planting work for the St. Louis Baptist Association.

Missouri WMU chose Laura Mason as the state centennial chairman in 1985, so 1986 was filled with preparation for the national WMU Centennial. Several associational and local WMU histories were written, and the state history was released in 1987 at the Annual Meeting in Jefferson City. As Missouri WMU began its new year in October 1986, it joined with others in preparation for the national WMU Centennial. Changes were made in programming in 1986. The GA Retreat, which was held in March, was once again overbooked, so two retreats were planned for 1987 to accommodate the large number of missions-minded GAs in the state. Camp Windermere for Girls was held for only two weeks in 1986 and was staffed by volunteers. Attendance had been dropping at Camp Windermere for Girls, so it became necessary to evaluate the state WMU camping program.

A new program for 1986 was an emphasis on creating Ethnic/Language and African-American

Southern Baptist WMU organizations. Loulla Efstathiou served as a consultant working with Ethnic/Language organizations. Virginia Clark was the consultant for African-American Southern Baptist organizations. This new realm of work extended the work of Missouri WMU beyond white, English-speaking women. This emphasis continued when four contract workers were obtained for 1987. At this time, there were two Ethnic/Language workers and two African-American Southern Baptist workers. St. Louis and Kansas City each had an Ethnic/Language worker and an African-American Southern Baptist worker to lead in the major metropolitan areas.

In 1987, there was no Camp Windermere for Girls planned, and emphasis was placed on associational camps. Another planned change was an alteration of the WMU Conference. For several years, women had been driving to Windermere to attend one day of the usual three-day sessions. In 1987, there was a special one-day session geared toward those who could not stay for a longer period. There was also a four-day session and a weekend session, allowing a variety of options from which to choose.

Barbara Bray wrote an update of MWMU history entitled *From Change to Challenge, A Continuation of the History of the Missouri Woman's Missionary Union from 1998-2007.* Barbara Bray lived a lifetime of fulfilling her passion for missions by leading

CHAPTER 20

conferences, writing for WMU magazines, and authoring two books for WMU. Barbara Bray left her earthly home at the age of 85 years old on January 15, 2006. Barbara was living at John Knox Village Care Center in Lee's Summit at the time of her passing. Her family rests in the assurance that the Lord met Barbara at the entrance of her eternal rest saying, "Well done you good and faithful servant." (Matthew 25:21a, Modern English Version)

CHAPTER 21

The Presidency of Norma Hays Altis

Missouri WMU President
1986-1991

At the April 4-5, 1986 Annual Meeting at First Baptist Church in Springfield, Mrs. Norma Altis was elected fourteenth President of the Missouri WMU because Barbara Bray had served her five-year term.

Norma Deloris Hays was born near McGirk, Missouri, on June 20, 1934, to Quincy and Letha Hays. She accepted Christ in June of 1943 at the Lebanon Baptist Church in McGirk and continued to be active in that church throughout her youth. Norma was educated at the Harlan School in Moniteau County and California, Missouri, high school. She married Hubert D. Altis on Easter Sunday, April 18, 1954, in Kansas City. Two sons were born to the

CHAPTER 21

family. Mrs. Altis continued a lifetime pattern of attention to her family and church. Her emphasis in WMU work was on Baptist Women, but she worked in all age levels except Mission Friends. Norma served her association as WMU Director and was the first woman to serve as moderator of an association in Missouri. She served as moderator of the Clay-Platte Association from 1979-1983. On the state WMU level, Mrs. Altis served on the Executive Committee from 1977-1980 as a member-at-large for Baptist Women. She then served as Vice-President from 1980-1985. Mrs. Altis served as WMU President from 1986-1991. While serving as Missouri's President, she also served as Missouri Vice-President to the national WMU.

Norma's dream was: *"that we can really 'double our mission vision' and enroll and involve many more women, girls, and preschoolers in the WMU organizations through our churches. I believe this is vital for the missions program of the SBC – Foreign and Home Missions."* [1]

A preliminary part of the state's celebration was the release of a history of Missouri Baptist Woman's Missionary organizations. *Ye Are the Branches,* written by Laura Mason, was presented to members of Missouri WMU at the April 10-11,1987, Annual Meeting at First Baptist Church, Jefferson City. This history covered the years up through the end of 1986. This occurred in the middle of the first year of Norma

Altis' presidency.

An important part of the Woman's Missionary Union is the relationships that are blended between members. This is especially true for those who serve on the state level. The joy of the centennial preparation was dulled by the death of Polly Hosler, Public Relations Coordinator on the Executive Committee, in late 1986. Polly's home association prepared a centennial quilt in her honor and presented it in her memory. The quilt was displayed at the Missouri WMU office at the Baptist Building.

A joyous event was the wedding of Debbie Bailey, Associate in the WMU Department, to Wood Miller. Debbie continued to work with women in WMU while Kathy Stahr worked with youth and children, and Alberta Gilpin, Executive Director, directed the entire Missouri WMU program with special attention to associational work.

The beginning of 1987 found Missouri WMU in the midst of preparation for the national WMU centennial celebration. Laura Mason had been trained as state centennial chairman. Associations and churches found willing women to serve as local chairmen. Statewide activities were being formulated: some came from ideas within the state, and other ideas came from national WMU.

In October 1986, the Executive Committee considered a request from national WMU to honor

Laura Armstrong. Plans were being made nationally to dedicate special grave markers for former national WMU Presidents. Since Laura Malotte Armstrong had been national WMU President from 1933 till her death on Mother's Day in 1945, plans proceeded to dedicate a marker at her graveside in Maryville in early 1987. This lovely ceremony took place immediately prior to the centennial Annual Meeting.

Programming in 1987 was examined, revised in some cases, and supported. Instead of week-long WMU Conferences, consideration was given to offering two-day, three-day, and one-day options. This gave women a variety of conference formats from which to choose, and the well-received idea garnered a total attendance of 882 women. The Baptist Young Women Encounter in April brought in 100 young women. A Baptist Nursing Fellowship chapter was organized for Missouri in March 1987, and 771 attended Teen Scene in the fall.

In 1987, the Annual Meeting at First Baptist Church, Jefferson City, was filled with anticipation of the upcoming centennial celebration. God was at work in other ways, too, because one of the speakers was Randy Sprinkle, missionary to Lesotho. A God-directed plan of prayer support was begun linking Missouri WMU and the southern African country of Lesotho. Women across the state began to "Lift Up Lesotho" under the guidance of former President

Marilyn Coble. The women's diligent prayers helped assure a Baptist witness in that mountain country encircled by South Africa.

Emphasis was placed on expanding WMU work. Two consultants already worked with African-American Southern Baptists, and two worked with language/ ethnic groups. Loulla Efstahiou and Minnie Collins worked in the Kansas City area, while Theresa Smith and Jane Garcia served in the greater St. Louis community. In 1987-88, WMU added three more consultants, which were financed by the Cooperative Program and worked across the state. The consultants were Opal Lantz, Eva Rauniker, and Erene Walker.

At the May 1987 Executive Committee Meeting, a missionary residence was suggested to be funded by the state missions offering. Many local churches and associations had missionary residences, and consideration was given to having a missionary residence in Jefferson City. Furloughing missionaries could give emphasis to the Cooperative Program and be available to speak to churches throughout Missouri.

There was not a Camp Windermere for Girls in 1987, but 1,875 attended the two GA Retreats in March. Response was enthusiastic to having an overnight stay at Windermere, where GAs could be immersed in a missions experience. Attitudes were upbeat, enthusiasm for missions was building, and all-in-all, Missouri WMU dwelt securely in Christ's

CHAPTER 21

mission on earth.

The year of the national WMU Centennial started joyously as staff member Kathy Stahr wed Joe Scott in January 1988. The year continued to roll along when 2,050 girls and leaders attended the three GA Retreats to establish a new tradition in Missouri WMU. In addition, over 500 girls attended Teen Scene that fall, over 600 women came to the three WMU Conferences, and more than 700 were trained at Regional and Associational WMU Training meetings.

Missions education and training were important parts of 1988, and so was giving. Three instances stand out to show the emphasis the women placed on giving. The first instance was when the WMU Executive Committee voted to start collecting a Madge N. Truex offering at Annual Meetings and at WMU Conferences. Prior to this time, income to the fund came at the initiative of the local churches and associations. The women responded by giving more enthusiastically to this important avenue of supporting special missions projects related to Missouri. The second giving opportunity was the renaming of the state missions offering to "Missouri Missions Offering." Efforts were renewed to make this an important ministry to the state, and Missouri WMU giving was displayed by those women participating in the bus trip to the national WMU Centennial Celebration in Richmond, Virginia. The third giving opportunity came on the return trip to Missouri as the women on the five busses were convicted of the need to collect money for the Lottie Moon Christmas Offering. Pleas had gone out to bolster the sagging offering, and the response was the ingathering of over $6,000. Sacrificial giving is just one response of those abiding in Christ and feeling secure.

The Centennial Celebration was an uplifting time for those involved. Emphasis was placed on the centennial during activities throughout the year. The highlight for Missouri women was the Annual Meeting held at Second Baptist Church in Liberty, April 15-16,1988. Those attending were blessed to hear from missionaries and Alma Hunt, former national WMU Executive Director. The attendees heard missions history through theme interpretations and dramatic performances. WMU members attending were inspired by speakers that testified to the productive heritage of WMU and the hope for a bright future for missions supporters.

The national Centennial Celebration in Richmond, Virginia, was a once-in-a-lifetime experience for those attending that event in May 1988. Missouri women packed five busses which rolled out to Virginia and back in an all-too-short trip. The experience changed lives and challenged all to further dedication to missions.

CHAPTER 21

It would be naïve to assume that all was well for Missouri WMU and national WMU. Times were unsettled for the Southern Baptist Convention as members squabbled over differing opinions and theology. WMU stressed its auxiliary status at all levels and tried to ride out the storm. This appeared to work for a time, but insecurity crept in when the women contemplated the future of the convention and WMU. Rather than cowering in fear or worry, Missouri WMU created a long-range planning committee to plan for the future. National WMU likewise, studied the past, present, and future to chart the best course through the troubled waters. Women throughout the nation and state did as they'd been taught when confronting threats to their missions organization, they prayed.

One aspect of the SBC controversy of concern was the stagnancy of income. The possibility of a 5% cut in the 1990 budget was brought up at the May Executive Committee Meeting. Missions offerings had been sagging, and the Cooperative Program was experiencing lower revenues. Financial reality set in during 1989, and programming vaporized when there was no money for implementation.

For Missouri WMU, established items were continued with some streamlining. Publications were reduced or eliminated. One example of this was the discontinuation of the *Outlook*. This periodical had been mailed to Missouri WMU leadership to inform and to instruct for many years. Upon consideration, it was decided that the best course of action was to combine MBC department publications into one news insert in the *Word and Way* entitled, *Communique*. This process change in 1990 provided information to a broader audience and encouraged increased subscriptions to the state's Baptist paper.

More financial scrutiny was given to ideas for new programming. There were new programs, but they were done with cost-effectiveness as a major factor. One new program was support for the missionary residence in Jefferson City. This home was purchased through Missouri Missions Offering funding. It was furnished through donations by churches and associations across the state. The WMU and Brotherhood organizations played a key role in furnishing the house.

Another new program was the creation of a Missouri Minister's Wives organization. This ministry tool was implemented with minimal cost to the WMU Department, so the organization was created in October 1990.

Acteen Activators was another program developed because it required little financial commitment by the WMU Department. Acteen Activators are groups of Acteens, generally from one church, who train and complete a special mission project in the US or

CHAPTER 21

abroad.

A special treat for Acteens was the trip to the national Acteens Convention (NAC) in San Antonio on July 12-15, 1989. Five busses of enthusiastic teens and leaders provided their own financial support for this trip which combined NAC with mission projects on the way. The program was worth the cost, and Missouri WMU tallied up yet another national event that could inspire and encourage.

An expansion of programming was the start-up of the Missionary Family Retreat on the first weekend in November. This ministry to missionary families funded by the Madge N. Truex Fund served a valuable purpose of fellowship and continued to be a favorite in the yearly calendar of activities.

Norma Altis faced the reality that 1990-91 was her last year as President since there is a five-year term limit for President. As she had done in the previous four years, Norma led Missouri WMU as it forged a missions future for the state as well as serving as Vice-President from Missouri on the national WMU Board. Alberta Gilpin, Debbie Miller, Kathy Scott, and Norma Altis gave guidance and wisdom in all deliberations at the national level.

Meanwhile, state work went on. GA Retreats flourished. In 1990 over 2,550 attended the three GA Retreats and one Mother/Daughter weekend. Twenty-six (including three men) went to Jericho, a missions conference, at Glorieta in July. Eight teams of Acteen Activators went out for short-term missionary service. Nearly 500 attended the three WMU Conferences at Windermere, and 80 attended the associational training.

The WMU family was saddened to learn of the deaths of two former Presidents and an Executive Secretary. Mrs. Louise McKee and Mrs. Lena Burnham, former Presidents, passed away in 1990. The former staff member who died that year was Mary O. Bidstrup, who had faithfully served Missouri WMU from 1948-1973. Their legacy of hard work, love of missions, and prayer commitment served as an example for those who knew them.

CHAPTER 22

The Presidency of Dawn O'Neill Phillips

Missouri WMU President
1991-1996

Dawn Phillips was elected as the fifteenth President of Missouri Woman's Missionary Union at the April 19-20, 1991 Annual Meeting at Harvester Baptist Church in St. Charles.

Dawn Carter O'Neill was born on November 6, 1950, at Missouri Baptist Hospital, to Rev. C.D. and Lucy O'Neill. Dawn was destined to be a mission advocate from the time she was a twinkling in her parents' eyes. C.D. was educated at Southern Seminary, and as was typical of many preachers' wives at the time, Lucy graduated from the WMU Training School in Louisville, KY. Dawn was born in a Baptist Hospital and has spent a majority of her life involved with Baptists, especially in Missouri WMU work, where her mother was a longtime Missouri Training School trustee. Christ became personal when Dawn accepted Him at age six and began maintaining a missions lifestyle. Dawn met Steven Phillips when both were students at Southwest Baptist College in Bolivar. She graduated with a bachelor's degree in 1972 and married Steven on August 13, 1972. Dawn became a pastor's wife and welcomed two sons to the family. Dedicated to missions, Dawn began her missions service in her church, association, the state, and national WMU.

The first of Dawn's duties as president was to help Missouri WMU Executive Committee adapt to a new framework. The long-range committee had offered its recommendations. The Executive Committee would still have a president, vice-president responsible for the Madge N. Truex Fund, a recording secretary, and members representing the various areas of the state and the different age-level organizations. The addition was a set of coordinators, which would direct subcommittees that would deal with mission action, missions growth, and missions support.

The Executive Committee met in May 1991, and great things began to come forth because of the better utilization of committee time. The Mary O. Bidstrup Scholarship was instituted to provide money for training and materials for churches that did not have

CHAPTER 22

an active WMU program. Four scholarships of $50 were awarded upon recommendation of Associational WMU Directors or Directors of Missions on a first come, first served basis. Another new ministry was one to missionary parents. Missouri WMU members "adopted" missionary parents in order to support them and their children. In an effort to strengthen Baptist Young Women work, Acteens who received Studiact scholarships from Missouri Baptist colleges were offered complimentary subscriptions to *Contempo* by Missouri WMU. MWMU chose prison ministry as the first statewide mission action emphasis. Through this ministry, countless lives were touched, and increasing numbers of Baptist Women became involved in mission action.

Traditional programming continued in 1991. The Camp Directors Workshop, which was begun soon after the demise of Camp Windermere for Girls, was held in January to train associational camp workers. About 2,300 people attended three GA Retreats. WMU training for associational directors was a part of Believe in Growth Missouri Associational Council (B.I.G M.A.C.), and the WMU Conference guided 505 women into the 1991-92 emphasis for WMU work. A GA Mother/Daughter weekend was held in August 1991, and 172 attended. The Missionary Family Retreat continued to be popular, and the Youth Missions Encounter inspired over 500 young people.

Kathy Scott was preparing to go to Ghana with a group of Acteen Activators from Missouri in the summer of 1992. At the October 1991 Executive Committee meeting, the group voted to give Kathy a $400 gift from the Madge N. Truex Fund in order to assist her in this endeavor. Once again, the Madge N. Truex Fund enabled funding for a special project.

The Madge N. Truex committee came to the rescue again at the April 1992 Annual Meeting. Wayne and Alice, missionaries to Lesotho, spoke at the meeting in Jefferson City. As a gift from Missouri WMU to help with their ministry in Lesotho, the Truex Fund supplied a communion set, cups, and a tablecloth for the Lord's Supper ordinance. The missionaries left a reminder of Lesotho with Missouri WMU by giving a lovely wall hanging from Lesotho.

The April 10-11, 1992 Annual Meeting was at First Baptist Church, Jefferson City. The meeting also served as a time to commemorate Alberta Gilpin's twenty-five years of service to Missouri WMU. The Friday evening session was devoted to praising God for the blessings and guidance she had given Missouri WMU. It was a festive time of remembering the past twenty-five years, which gave hope for God's continued benevolence in the future.

Missouri WMU didn't and never has existed in a vacuum. The controversy in the SBC continued and impacted work on the national and state level. An

CHAPTER 22

atmosphere of diminished trust and trepidation became the environment for many Southern Baptists. Most of the brunt was felt by national WMU as it faced takeover threats. Alberta Gilpin served on the committee to help national WMU to focus on its direction. A special informative session was held at the 1992 Annual Meeting, and Alberta Gilpin spoke to those attending from her heart about the controversy and its impact to WMU. It was a difficult time of thought and consideration for WMUers. Regardless of what might happen to the beloved WMU, nothing could diminish the permanence of commitment between Christ and the women who showed their love through missions dedication.

Thought and planning went into everything related to WMU and all aspects of Baptist life. As a result of this process, evidence of reorganization and fine-tuning was revealed. One such example was the reorganization of the department in the MBC, which deals with WMU. A team approach was suggested, which borrowed practices from current business practices and theories of interpersonal dynamics. Following prayerful and judicious consideration, the plan was endorsed by Missouri WMU.

WMU work continued as women channeled their energies into what could be done, and that resulted in novel approaches to missions. The missions growth committee proposed the Missouri Emeritus Missionary Biography series as a way to honor retired missionaries by sharing the story of their lives and to inspire others in the missions endeavor. Each year three or four missionaries have had biographies written about them, presented to them at Annual Meeting, and enjoyed by Missouri WMU members.

The needs of prisoners and their families was so great that the mission action emphasis was continued into 1992. The Madge N. Truex committee endeavored to encourage gifts to the fund by providing associations with awards for giving based on per capita donations for three sizes of associations. The whole executive committee instituted prayer partners in order to strengthen each other through prayer and improved relationships.

Missouri WMU programming continued to draw in attendees. The three GA Retreats had over 2,500 in attendance, over 500 came to Teen Scene, and the revised WMU Conference brought in 669. The revision to the WMU conference was the addition of associational training at the state conference rather than through regional training meetings. The associational training didn't take the entire conference time, so participants could also benefit from other WMU conference sessions and speakers.

While Missouri leadership was primarily concerned with state work, participation in national WMU governing bodies required action by the

Missouri President and the staff. Missouri Presidents and staff have established themselves as wise contributors to national WMU governance, and this was especially true as the national body considered how to deal with the troubling environment. This filtered down in 1992 to Missouri WMU Executive Committee when it met in special session to compose a tribute of support for national WMU. Taking a strong stand for national WMU to remain an Auxiliary could have brought repercussions for Missouri WMU, but the main response of fellow Missouri Baptists was admiration for such a clear stand.

In the state arena, missions emphasis continued. In 1992, a new state mission action focus stressed the needs of migrants and creative ways for local and associational WMUs to respond. Response was good for programming too, as members came in force to the three GA Retreats, WMU Conference with association and church training tracks, and Youth Missions Encounter.

The April 16-17, 1993, Annual Meeting was a special one for recognizing two of Missouri's beloved leaders: Madge N. Truex and Laura M. Armstrong. At Raytown First Baptist Church, two new pamphlets about Truex and Armstrong were released to the public. Once again, Missouri WMU found strength for the present by looking at the strength of those in the past.

Missouri WMU leaders were on the move in 1993. Norma Tolbert and Laura Mason were designated as Resource Representatives by the national WMU and were trained in Birmingham on how to encourage increased sales of national products. Since national WMU receives most of its funding from sales of periodicals and materials, these two women worked throughout the state to increase sales and thus increase the national budget.

Missouri Baptists began a five-year partnership in October 1993 with the country of Belarus and the state of Wyoming. Missourians were challenged to go "Beyond Our Borders," and a concentrated effort was started to link Missouri with Belarus and Wyoming. Debbie Miller traveled to Belarus in late 1993 to investigate ways that Missouri WMU could assist sisters in Belarussian churches. Debbie's preliminary trip, under the encouragement of the Baptist World Alliance Women's Department, led to wonderful opportunities in 1994.

The Missouri WMU held its Annual Meeting at Hannibal LaGrange College on April 15-16, 1994. This choice was made in an effort to take MBC programming to various corners of the state in order to encourage attendance. MBC programming was planned so that a major meeting would be held in different locations each year. Missouri WMU complied, but it soon became evident that there were few locations in Missouri with sufficient accommodations for the WMU Annual Meeting, MBC Evangelism Conference, or the Missouri Baptist Convention.

One of the highlights of the Hannibal Annual Meeting was the tremendous response to the mission action project, which requested materials be brought for migrant kits. Those in charge of gathering the material were overwhelmed when 2,000 health kits were assembled. This far exceeded the needs of those working with migrants in the state, so the surplus was shared with home missionaries working in multi-housing units.

GA Retreats grew in 1994. Another weekend was included so that there were almost 1,700 attending the four weekends of GA Retreats. The highlight of the year for 362 Acteens was the national Acteens Convention (NAC) held in Birmingham, Alabama.

The partnership with Belarus women grew in 1994 as plans began to take shape for a national Women's Meeting in Minsk in 1995. In order to work out the details of this meeting, four Missouri WMU leaders traveled to Belarus. They were Dawn Phillips, Barbara Popp, Margaret Harrelson, and Debbie Miller. Once again, Madge Truex Fund supported Missouri WMU through the provision of $600 to assist with expenses of the trip.

A revision was made to the framework for state mission action projects during the 1994-1995 year. Instead of one focus ministry, the committee decided to emphasize different projects for each of the four quarters of the year. In order to improve communication about these varied programs, the committee began a quarterly Mission Action Newsletter that was distributed to associational WMU directors for dissemination to local leaders.

Various means of record keeping have been used through the years, but all seemed unreliable as a true measurement of membership or involvement in WMU. In order to obtain funding from MBC, it became more and more necessary to show that there really was a large audience benefiting from the expenditures. Justification of budgets has continually been a concern for Missouri WMU. In 1992, Missouri WMU began considering a registration fee for those attending Annual Meeting. The nominal fee was accepted without much uproar, and attendance didn't seem to decrease because of the fee. This paved the way for a unique Annual Meeting ministry in 1995.

At the suggestion of Alberta Gilpin, the Executive Committee decided that the 1995 Annual Meeting be a one-day meeting held on April 29 at First Baptist Church, Jefferson City. This abbreviated meeting would be a commissioning service for those women going to Belarus for the national women's meeting at

CHAPTER 22

the end of May. The final aspect was that the registration fees received from the Annual Meeting be used as scholarships to enable Belarussian women leaders to attend the meeting in Minsk. Financial necessity in a normal year gave way to an opportunity to minister to others in a unique situation.

Eighty-six women and three men made the trip to Belarus in May 1995 to help Belarussian partners develop a Baptist Women's program. The trip was a learning experience, an opportunity to appreciate God's blessings, and a chance to minister. Many who went thought they were going to minister and realized afterward that they were the recipients of the ministry from their Belarussian sisters. Those who have gone through trying times have much to teach others.

The Belarus trip caused most Missouri WMU women to reconsider their priorities. One who examined her life after the trip to Belarus was Debbie Miller, who submitted her resignation in the fall of 1995. Her decision to be a full-time mother was admired by most. A new relationship that developed was that between Wood and Debbie Miller and their adopted son, Olin. Olin came into their lives in January of 1994. The benefit was that even though Debbie was no longer a salaried employee that didn't restrict her from being a volunteer like everyone else.

The Wyoming/MBC partnership had ramifications for Missouri WMU, too. Because Wyoming is

150

relatively close compared to Belarus, it is difficult to tally up the efforts undertaken, which related to WMU. Leadership teams wanted to assist with training, Acteen Activators helped with GA programming, and many local and associational groups worked to strengthen WMU work in Wyoming. As is the case with the Belarus partnership, Missouri WMU members learned that pioneer women from the wide-open spaces can teach and inspire as much if not more than those from Missouri.

Missouri WMU programming continued to receive support in 1995. The only programming change was that there were three regular GA Retreats in March, and the last weekend was designated as a Mother/Daughter Retreat. Over 2,400 participated in GA Retreats. Attendance was somewhat lower for WMU Conference, but this probably relates to the expense and time involved in the Belarus trip.

Fall of 1995 instituted yet another change in programming at the national WMU. "The only constant is change" could be the bywords of the 1990s. Like Missouri WMU, the national organization had felt the need to accurately measure WMU membership and to provide adequate financing for desired programming. This led to changes in the national organization format. Mission action became missions involvement, Baptist Women and Baptist Young Women became Women on Mission, *Royal*

CHAPTER 22

Service became *Missions Mosaic*, membership in WMU was redefined, and other changes came about. A national missions involvement emphasis (AIDS) was started also.

These changes at the national level influenced Missouri WMU. State leaders were trained in the new format so that local and associational leaders could be trained. This resulted in the training of new special workers who joined the ranks of experienced leaders. The WMU Executive Committee revised the bylaws in order to accommodate new terminology and ideas, but all in all, the changes were well received because of good communication, openness, and renewed trust.

Dawn Phillips completed her five years of service as President at the Annual Meeting in Cape Girardeau in 1996. Dawn didn't rest on her laurels, though, because at the Missouri WMU Council meeting prior to the Annual Meeting, she presented a proposed partnership with the city of Tianjin in China. This was accepted by Missouri WMU, and Dawn led in using Missouri WMUs fine-tuned prayer power to aid those representing Christ in this closed country and unreached city.

The Altis and Phillips years were over, and Missouri WMU waited expectantly as Barbara Popp assumed the presidency.

CHAPTER 23
The Presidency of Barbara Daniels Popp

Missouri WMU President
1996-1999

Barbara Daniels was born on November 15, 1937, to W.H. (Bill) and Kathryn Daniels. Barbara was born in Red Oak, Iowa, and then lived with her family in Oklahoma before they moved to Cape Girardeau, Missouri. Barbara accepted Christ at age eleven at the First Baptist Church in Cape Girardeau. Barbara was active in WMU as a GA and continued on through Young Women's Auxiliary, Campus YWA, Baptist Women, and Women on Mission. She graduated from Central High in Cape Girardeau and attended Southeast Missouri State University prior to marrying John W. Popp in May 1957. Barbara and John welcomed two sons and a daughter to their marriage. Barbara

CHAPTER 23

devoted her time to her family, her church, and to community service through the General Federation of Women's Clubs (GFWC). Barbara's leadership skills were enhanced through work in WMU, Sunday School, and GFWC, in which she served as Missouri President from 1988-1990 and served for six years on the GFWC national board. Within WMU, Barbara served in numerous capacities in the local church, association, and the state. Barbara served on the WMU Executive Committee as an Area Six representative and served as Vice-President for five years. She was elected President of Missouri WMU in April 1996 at First Baptist Church, Cape Girardeau. Her leadership experience helped create an atmosphere where Missouri WMU could flourish.

Barbara Popp said, "When I accepted Jesus Christ as my Lord and Savior, He gave me a heart for missions! I have always been drawn to women who share that same passion. I began attending Missouri WMU Annual Meetings and met Alberta Gilpin, but only knew her 'from afar.' She was always on the platform with the President and other program personnel mostly making announcements, but I quickly sensed she, too, had a heart for missions! When she *prayed,* I recall thinking, 'Here is a woman who also believes in the power of prayer!' There was something about her prayers that made me know she had a close walk with God!"

A special treat for those attending the 1996 Annual Meeting in Cape Girardeau was the Foreign Mission Board Commissioning Service for Foreign Missionaries during the Saturday afternoon session. Missouri WMU members enjoyed the bonuses of having a larger number of missionaries present, showing cooperation with the Board, and taking part in the send-off of more beloved missionaries.

While Missouri WMU was flourishing, it was still not a peaceful world in the SBC. A proposal was presented to restructure the operating units of the convention. The restructuring was to begin in 1998. Proponents said that the new structure would be more cost-efficient and effective. It would prepare the convention to meet the new century. Opponents were distressed at the elimination of some programs and the absorption of others by different programs. The changes moved through the channels in 1996. WMU members were concerned, but the impact was not immediate since the national WMU remained an independent auxiliary to the SBC.

Partnerships were an important part of Missouri WMU in 1996. The women had nine years of prayer support for Lesotho, three years of partnership with Belarus and Wyoming, and were beginning a faith journey of prayer with those working in Tianjin.

Another faith journey was taken by those participating in the study committee of Missouri WMU.

CHAPTER 23

Their challenge was to develop a vision for WMU which would guide it into the next century. Once the vision was determined, decisions on structure and programming were made. One decision resulted in the proposed restructuring of the WMU Executive Committee. The restructuring plan was presented to the Executive Committee in 1997 and was voted on at the 1998 Annual Meeting in Raytown. When approved, this resulted in a new subcommittee within the Executive Committee which was devoted to preserving Missouri WMU history. This was under the direction of the Recording Secretary.

In 1996, a decision was made to increase the number of Mary O. Bidstrup scholarships from four to eight. Interest in these new WMU work funds had been increasing each year, so providing eight scholarships helped bolster WMU work in churches that had none.

Cindy Still became part of Missouri WMU in early 1997 when she assumed the responsibility for adult women. Cindy came to Missouri with expertise in WMU, singles ministry, and women's ministry. She helped Missouri WMU stretch and expand in new directions in order to include all women and children with an interest in missions.

The Executive Committee directed missions involvement work now instead of mission action. With this change in the works, the mission support committee changed its name to more clearly reflect its purpose: missionary ministries. Missions involvement efforts resulted in 1,500 packets being delivered to the Boonville Correction Center in December 1996 from churches and associations across the state. Child advocacy was the national missionary ministry emphasis for 1996-97, and Missouri WMU developed guidelines to assist women in making a difference in the lives of children around them.

A new project of the missionary ministry committee was to assure that all home and foreign missionaries who considered Missouri as home would receive copies of *PrayerWays*. Local churches adopted missionaries and mailed copies of this monthly prayer guide to them so the missionaries could pray for colleagues and know of the needs that were bathed in prayer by Missouri Baptist women.

The new national WMU format was received well by the women of Missouri. Numerous testimonies came forth about keeping the status quo under the new Women on Mission framework and adding new groups for those who had previously not considered themselves as members of WMU. The missions involvement committee began to record these success stories, and started publishing a quarterly newsletter like the one done by the missionary ministry committee. These two newsletters served to inform and encourage participation so that Missouri WMU

CHAPTER 23

work could grow and flourish.

A continued encouragement was the response to GA Retreats. In 1996, over 2,800 participated in the four weekend retreats in March. As these GAs grow, the challenge was to keep them involved in a missions lifestyle rather than losing them as had happened with previous generations.

Preparations were begun for the celebration of seventy-five years of Missouri WMU in 1996. A committee made plans for the activities of the anniversary, which were initiated at the October 1997 MBC Convention and continued to the end of 1998.

Missouri WMU members met at Springfield First Baptist Church in April 18-19,1997, to begin the second year of the Popp presidency. The meeting was informative, inspirational, and challenging as in years past. The women were delighted to honor former Presidents and retired staff members. Those in attendance were recognized, and greetings were sent to those unable to attend. Retired staff present were Adele Maness and Nell Constantz. Former Presidents in attendance were: Viola Scherff, Marilyn Coble, Lorene Murphy, Barbara Bray, Norma Altis, and Dawn Phillips. These women served as an inspiration and mentors to younger members.

An added bonus of this Annual Meeting was recognition of Alberta Gilpin's thirtieth anniversary with Missouri WMU. Unbeknownst to Alberta, a love offering was gathered from women across the state to be divided evenly between Alberta and the Madge N. Truex Fund. A brief celebration was held at the conclusion of the Friday evening session. It was a special moment for all when Alberta was recognized and presented with a monetary gift for herself and one in her name to the Madge N. Truex Fund. Alberta thanked the ladies for being so generous and gracious, but the ladies knew that no one had been as generous with her life and love or as gracious to all as Alberta.

A high point of 1997 was the announcement that the Uniform Church Letters in Missouri showed an increase in WMU membership. This was a reversal to a longtime trend of decreasing membership, so WMU leadership celebrated and thanked God for this new growth. Numbers were up for WMU membership! The missions involvement committee was busy developing a record-keeping system that would show what is done in churches and associations across the state. Forms were given out at the Believe in Growth Missouri Associational Councils (BIG MAC) meeting in May 1997, and leaders were anxious to see what the response would be.

BIG MAC associational training at Windermere had a new slant to it in 1997 when WMU Area representatives were invited to play a more important part in discussions and planning with associational leaders. This strengthened the team effort of Missouri

CHAPTER 23

WMU.

Missouri WMU was hostess to a national WMU Regional Training session in September 1997. This meeting was a result of the discontinuance of WMU Training at Glorieta and Ridgecrest. Women from throughout the Midwest gathered at Windermere to learn from national WMU representatives. A regional meeting had been held in Illinois in 1996, and a group of new Missouri leaders attended this meeting for training and then brought back their expertise for the 1997 WMU Conference. The pool of trained special workers in Missouri WMU was growing.

A change took place in 1997 when Special Workers met at Windermere in the new lodge facilities in August. Traditionally, Special Worker training had taken place in January. The changed format was accepted readily, and many of the women enjoyed being able to stay on at Windermere for WMU Conference.

Giving increased to the Cooperative Program and to special offerings in 1997. It was easier to flourish when the funds were pouring in.

One challenge in 1997 was to retrain Baptists in the terminology that came about from the approved restructuring in the SBC. The Foreign Mission Board became the International Mission Board. The Home Mission Board expanded its coverage to be the North American Mission Board. Uncertainty reigned as the

The Presidency of Barbara Daniels Popp

process evolved to reveal what would happen to Brotherhood programming since it became the responsibility of the North American Mission Board.

There were two new staff members who joined the WMU team. Gwen Martin joined as a secretary, and Cindy Still was welcomed in July 1997 to work with Women on Mission as well as other duties related to the Missions Education and Ministry Development Team.

On a personal note, Joe and Kathy Scott worked through the process of adopting a child from China. God provided a son, David, that the couple brought into their family around Labor Day, 1997. David was a constant reminder of Missouri WMU's partnership with Tianjin and its long-term love of Chinese that goes back to Lottie Moon.

The beginning of 1998 brought anticipation about the 75th anniversary of Missouri WMU. The four GA Retreats in March included an emphasis on Missouri WMU history. There were 2,950 who attended the GA retreats. There were 1,230 boys registered at RA Congress, plus 125 volunteers. Missouri WMU's total enrollment was 33,610.

WMU members were challenged to *Come, Go with Me* at the April 17-18, 1998, Annual Meeting held at First Baptist Church, Raytown. Dellanna O'Brien, national WMU Executive Director, and Alma Hunt, a former national WMU Executive Director, were at

CHAPTER 23

that meeting. Each session began with a skit challenging attenders to "Go!" There were 863 registered at the meeting. There were four WMU members present at the 75th Anniversary who had been members of Missouri WMU for the last 75 years.

The missionary speakers were Brian and Rose from Indonesia and Jim and Grace, agricultural missionaries from Haiti. Dellanna O'Brien spoke of the new century and challenged the participants to grow spiritually, become prayer warriors, sharpen their skills, keep focused on children, welcome diversity in age and ethnics, and stress evangelism. Victor and Nina Krutko asked members of the audience to "come and go" with them to Belarus. Nina spoke of the love Belarusian women had for Missouri Baptists, and Victor requested prayer for religious freedom in Belarus. Alberta urged women to pray for 99 women who would go to the Belarusian Women's meeting in May. Missionary Kids, Billy and Ann Bowers, expressed thanks for the support given to their parents, Bill and Carol Bowers, IMB missionaries to Romania.

On Saturday afternoon, the Annual Meeting moved to the Mabee Center at William Jewell for a banquet, a highlight of MWMU's 75th anniversary celebration. The banquet program included a style show of fashions during the last 75 years. A presentation of a plaque commemorating the 75th anniversary of the Missouri Woman's Missionary Union was given by Jerry Cain, representing the Missouri Baptist Historical Commission. Alma Hunt recounted her relationship with Missouri Baptists as Dean of Women at William Jewell and told of the impact it had on her development. An offering was received for the Madge Truex Fund of $1,670.70, and $1,237.26 was given to the Wyoming/Belarus partnership offering.

The 76th Annual WMU Meeting was held at First Baptist Church in Jefferson City, April 17, 1999. It was a very special meeting, even though it was only a one-day meeting. Alberta had suggested to Barbara Popp, "Why don't we give the women of Belarus our Annual Meeting?" The decision was made to have a one-day Annual Meeting in order to have the money to finance a WMU meeting for the women in Belarus. Five hundred women attended, and they brought hundreds of gifts for the Belarussian women.

The theme of the meeting was "A Time to Go Beyond Our Borders." Wanda Lee, national WMU President, presented the theme interpretation dealing with Christians being the hand of God. She challenged the attendees to move beyond the ordinary boundaries of their lives and do great and mighty things. There was a special recognition of Acteens. Kathy Scott shared about national Acteens Convention (NAC) in 1998 at Louisville, Kentucky,

CHAPTER 23

where 11,000 were in attendance. Three hundred seventy Missouri girls and their leaders attended.

The women were invited to a Tea Party for lunch, where there was a reception to honor Barbara Popp, who was retiring as President. This was a surprise for Barbara, with the women bringing all the food and decorations for this celebration. Barbara presented a talk on "What is the Challenge of a New Millennium for Missouri WMU?" based on Jeremiah 29:11. Appropriately, a recording of a Belarussian Choir served as pre-session music before the afternoon meeting. Martha, who was currently staying in the missionary residence in Jefferson City, asked the women, "What borders do we need to cross?" She talked of the border of "fear" and how it can paralyze a person. She challenged the women present to work together to find victory for common problems and concerns. Barbara Popp announced that the meeting would depart from the printed program to create a video for the women of Belarus. Although it was deemed that now was not a good time for Missouri women to go to the Belarussian WMU meeting, Debbie Miller prayed that Missouri WMU could go to Belarus June 2000.

In 1999, 1,385 Royal Ambassadors and their leaders attended RA Congress. There were 45 decisions for Christ at that event.

Barbara Popp served as WMU President until 1999 when she chose not to let her name be presented for nomination for a fourth term. Barbara's earthly life ended on July 18, 2022. The reading of the daily Missionary Prayer Calendar was included at her memorial service.

CHAPTER 24

The Presidency of Debbie Bailey Miller

Missouri WMU President
1999-2004

At the 76th Annual WMU Meeting held at First Baptist Church in Jefferson City on April 17, 1999, was when Debbie Miller was elected as the 17th President of Missouri WMU. This was truly God's work as Debbie charted the waters of the many choices Missouri WMU had to make. Debbie had worked for the WMU Department for 17 years until her resignation in 1995 to spend more time with her family. During Debbie's five-year tenure as President, she worked with three WMU Executive Directors – Alberta Gilpin, Kathy Scott, and Vivian McCaughan.

Debbie was born on October 2, 1950, in Ardmore, Oklahoma, to Johnnie and Vonzene Bailey. She became a Christian at the age of seven in Tulsa,

Oklahoma. When Debbie was in 4th grade, her family moved to Midwest City, Oklahoma, and she attended Soldier Creek Baptist Church. As a young child, Debbie went with her mother to Woman's Missionary Society meetings. Debbie grew up going to Sunbeams and GAs. She moved through the Forward Steps in GAs to reach Queen with a Scepter and then graduated to YWAs. After high school, Debbie attended Oklahoma Baptist University and graduated in 1972 with a degree in English/Secondary Education. She attended Southwestern Baptist Theological Seminary in Fort Worth, Texas, and graduated in 1976 with a Master's in Religious Education. She worked with the St. Louis Baptist Association from June 1976 until July 1978 as WMU Promotional Director. From August 1978 until December 1995, she worked with the Missouri Baptist Convention as Baptist Women and Baptist Young Women Director, as a missions consultant for women/children, then as an Associate. She had numerous job titles during the 17 years she worked with MWMU. Then she met Wood Miller, and they were married in 1986. They adopted a son, Olin, in January of 1994.

In the year 2000, 3,157 girls attended GA Retreats. There were 1,300 registered for the RA Congress in Sedalia. The total WMU enrollment that year was 26,574. Cindy Still left the WMU staff and

CHAPTER 24

moved to California after serving Missouri WMU for three and a half years.

The theme for the 77th Annual Meeting was "Be Strong in the Lord and Be of Good Courage." It was held at Fee Fee Baptist Church in Bridgeton April 28-29, 2000. Pastor Randy Fullerton welcomed the ladies to the oldest Protestant church west of the Mississippi.

The music for the meeting was led by Carmela B., missionary in Moldova. Carmela told of her likeness to a Missouri mule and how God has used her courage in service to him in Benin and Moldova. Missionary Debbie Cannada shared how her husband shows "good courage" as he lives and ministers in his large inner-city community.

Gene and Jean P. spoke with the women about "He Will Protect You in Lesotho." Gene shared about the experience they had when kidnapped by four men around February 1, 1999, and the peace they felt in the midst of fear. They knew that God was with them and thanked Missouri WMU for praying for them unceasingly. Missionaries and WMU are a team together with WMU holding the ropes while the missionaries serve. Later, Jean shared that her only daughter and husband have been in Campus Crusade in Lesotho. On May 21, Beth and Wes and their three children were appointed as IMB missionaries to Lesotho.

Karen and Jerry C. are Missourians appointed to

Antigua. Before answering the call to Antigua, Karen served on the Missouri WMU Executive Committee. Karen told how she hates water. Through hurricanes and volcanoes, they related how God's protection is tied to "position (child of the King), possessions, and posture (kneeling in prayer)." Resting in the arms of Jesus is like being in the eye of a storm. We can live in the calm.

At the close of this meeting, Debbie Miller and Alberta Gilpin led in a commissioning service for seventy-six women going to Belarus in May 28-June 8, 2000. Debbie Miller reported the following in her President's Report for 2001: "As we met with our Baptist sisters in Belarus in June of 2000, we rejoiced that we were participating in a meeting planned and conducted by the Belarussian women. What a joy to see the growth of the national Baptist Women's Union of Belarus. Missouri WMU was able to give $3,000 for the support of Baptist Women's work in our partnership country because of the generous gifts of Missouri WMU."

After more than 33 years, Alberta Gilpin retired on December 31, 2000. (Alberta's story was told in Chapter 17.). Kathy Scott became Missouri WMU director in 2001. (See Chapter 25 for more information about Kathy.) Vivian McCaughan was named Missions Mobilization Initiative Coordinator on the Missouri Baptist Convention staff. Vivian has a

CHAPTER 24

strong WMU heritage and so her involvement with and support of WMU was anticipated. (See Chapter 26 for more information about Vivian). Missouri women would not be disappointed.

During 2001, there were 2,700 registered for GA Retreats. The GAs collected items that filled 66 infant care baskets that were delivered to Crisis Pregnancy Centers all over the state. Thirteen hundred registered for RA Congress at Sedalia, where 50 decisions were made to follow Christ. That year the Missouri WMU enrollment was 25,045 members. In the spring, a monthly WMU prayer calendar was reinstated in *Word and Way*.

The 78th Annual Meeting was held at South Haven Baptist Church in Springfield on April 20-21, 2001, with 700 in attendance. Ministry projects that the women participated in at the meeting included packaging towels and washcloths to be used at Grand Oaks Mission, working at a Habitat for Humanity House, helping feed and serve drinks to residents of the Baptist Home in Ozark, and serving lunch to homeless people in Springfield.

The theme was "Beyond Belief!" Janet Hoffman, President of the national WMU, gave the theme interpretation. Katsia M. shared about Belarus. She and her husband were students at Midwestern Seminary. At that time, her mother was the President of the Baptist Women's Union in Belarus. The churches there are called Houses of Prayer. The churches in Belarus pray for the Missouri churches they are linked with. Gayle Leininger shared about literacy work in Gatlinburg. Tennessee. She talked about how literacy classes reach people. When she had a literacy class in Orlando, Florida, one Cuban student came. She asked him, "If you have any friends or neighbors who want to learn English, bring them to our next class." There were 39 waiting on the stairs and porch the next time they met. This class grew to 170 Cubans. She shared many stories about the people who became Christians through literacy classes.

The Missouri WMU Leadership Team voted to incorporate WMU in September 2001. This made MWMU a 501(c)(3) status as a not-for-profit corporation. The Missouri WMU web pages were established. This site listed WMU leadership and provided a calendar of WMU events. The web address is www.mobaptist.org/wmu.

Memorial Baptist Church, Columbia, hosted the 79th Annual Meeting of Missouri WMU on April 12-13, 2002. The theme was "I Stand Amazed." Missionary speakers were Bill and Carol Bowers, who were on stateside assignment from Romania. Carol reminded attendees that missionaries are just like them, seeking to serve God where He has placed them. Liz L., missionary to Belarus, was stateside on furlough. Liz brought greetings from Belarus and asked for prayer

CHAPTER 24

for her and her husband to have vision, health, safety, and warmth when they returned overseas. She asked prayer for the home schooling of her daughters, for the lost, and for the Christians in Belarus.

On Friday evening, Willene Pierce, missionary to the Native American Link in Oklahoma, spoke about "LINK" ("Living in Neighborly Kindness"). One of Willene's most interesting efforts has been the women's choir which started with 50 women singing at the Oklahoma WMU meeting. As a result, 130 women from 16 different tribes sang at the national WMU meeting in St. Louis in June 2002.

The mission project during the Annual Meeting in Columbia included the gathering of items for hospitality bags to be used in Crossover St. Louis Kindness Explosion in June.

In 2002, the Missouri Acteens Retreat was held with 330 in attendance. Five young women made professions of faith during the event. In the fall of 2002, three Missourians, Zeldean Munton, Janet Dyer, and Janet Buchanan, traveled to Lesotho for a prayer walk and mission trip. GA Retreats had over 2,400 girls plus their counselors in attendance. There were 1,100 boys and counselors who attended the RA Congress, where over 150 decisions were made to follow Christ.

At the 2003 MWMU board meeting January 31-February 1, the following core values were adopted.

CORE VALUES

(1) We believe the Biblical mandate of the Great Commission is the responsibility of all believers.
(2) We believe in the core values and missions statement of WMU SBC.
(3) We believe in the importance of missions education for Baptist churches in Missouri.
(4) We believe in the importance of missions prayer partnerships.
(5) We believe in the support of Missouri missionaries.
(6) We believe in perpetuating a missions lifestyle.
(7) We believe in the development of missions leadership in Missouri.

The 80th Annual Meeting met at William Jewell College in Liberty on April 25-26, 2003. The theme was "God's Plan...My Part." Brenda Poinsett, MWMU Women's Ministry Specialist, spoke during the three general sessions on "God's Plan." Special guests were WMU sisters from Puerto Rico, Martha Aponte, President of the Puerto Association WMU, and Magali Candelorea, Association Secretary. Missionary speakers were Ken Welborn, NAMB Chaplain to the United Nations, Mary, Journeyman, and Wanda Lee, national WMU Executive Director. Wanda Lee gave the theme interpretation at the end of each of the general sessions.

Dixie Thornton, Missouri WMU Preschool Specialist, led Mission Friends organizations across

Missouri to collect quarters to purchase a water purifier for Missouri IMB missionaries Don and Diane C. A total of $1,738 was received from Mission Friends.

During the 2003 meeting, approximately 208 Missouri Baptist Girls in Action participated in Mission projects and learned from missionaries at the GA event held during the WMU Annual Meeting. In addition, there were 400 adults registered for this 2003 Annual Meeting. During that same year, three regional GA Retreats were held, and over 300 girls attended, and fourteen girls made professions of faith.

In 2004, the WMU enrollment was 31,067. There were six regional GA Retreats, and over 975 girls and leaders attended. Part of the GA retreat emphasis was the 90th birthday of GAs. RA Congress had 848 in attendance. There were 94 decisions, and 81 of the decisions were professions of faith. Three hundred twenty Missouri Acteens and leaders traveled to Synchronations, the national Acteens Convention. The Missouri Acteens Retreat was held in November 2004 at Hannibal-LaGrange College, with over 360 Acteens and their leaders participating. At this retreat, ten girls made professions of faith or decided to go into missions work.

"It's All about Missions" was the theme of the 81st Annual Meeting of Missouri WMU in Poplar Bluff on April 23-24, 2004. There were 360 adults registered for the meeting. Leota Pratt shared about her volunteer experience in Romania. Prayers were said for a group of Missourians who were in Romania at that time.

Several missionaries shared their experiences. Peggy and Bob spoke on their ministry to the deaf in Ecuador. Bonita, missionary from Southeast Asia and Oceania, invited the attendees to fly around the world with her visiting several areas where she served. Dora Narvaez shared about the Puerto Rico partnership, and Lucy Wagner spoke about her recent trip to the Korean WMU Anniversary. She was a missionary in South Korea for 38 years. NAMB Missionaries Jeff and Kim Moore spoke on their church planting ministry in Ohio.

Debbie's five years as State WMU President was recognized with a reception following the evening session. Debbie closed out the meeting by speaking on "Missions-Our Call, Our Focus, God's Command." She quoted Wanda Lee, who said, "WMU has had one significant purpose in its entire history-missions." (used with permission from Wanda Lee.) Debbie concluded by saying, "God commands us to be on mission for Him," something she practiced until her death. Debbie Bailey Miller passed away in her home in Jefferson City, Missouri, on June 11, 2022.

CHAPTER 25

The Leadership of Kathy Stahr Scott

WMU Executive Director
2001-2003

After the retirement of Alberta Gilpin on December 31, 2000, Kathy Scott became the eighth Missouri WMU Executive Director on January 1, 2001.

Kathy Stahr was born in St. Louis on June 19, 1958, to Tom and Dixie Stahr. She was their firstborn child, and later, she had three younger sisters. Kathy grew up attending First Baptist Church, St. John, in St. Louis. She received Jesus in her heart at nine years old. Kathy grew up in the mission organizations attending Sunbeams, GAs, and Acteens. She achieved Queen Regent in Service, the highest Acteen achievement. Kathy also participated in Training Union, choir, youth activities, and mission trips. At the age of 15, Kathy felt a call to missions. Kathy graduated from Ritenour high school, St. Louis, in 1976. Then she attended Oklahoma Baptist University in Shawnee from 1976-1980 and received a Bachelor of Arts degree in Sociology. In 1982, she attended Midwestern Theological Seminary. She graduated in 1985 with a Master's in Religious Education with an emphasis in Church Music.

Kathy began working for the Missouri Baptist Convention in January 1986 as a WMU Associate for Children/Youth. She also took on the Weekday Early Education aspect of ministries for the Missouri Baptist Convention. Kathy enjoyed planning many retreats and weekend training events for preschool leaders, Girls in Action and their leaders, and Acteens. She took Acteens to serve in MBC's partnership states, to national Acteens Conventions, and to Ghana for a mission trip. Kathy helped twice with the trips Missouri Baptist women took to Belarus during their partnership with the Missouri Baptist Convention.

Kathy met her husband, Joe Scott when he began working as a journalist for *Word and Way*, the state Baptist paper. Joe and Kathy were married in January 1989. In 1997, Kathy and Joe adopted their oldest son, David, from Wuhan province of China. In 2002, Kathy and Joe's second son Riley, was born in St. Louis.

CHAPTER 25

Kathy served as WMU Director and GA leader at various churches in her lifetime. Kathy said, "I benefited greatly and grew under the leadership of many of our women, Missouri Baptist Convention employees, and especially Alberta Gilpin and Debbie Miller."

Kathy worked with the WMU board and committees to further the work with missionaries, training leaders, planning and implementing state WMU meetings. Kathy was part of the Missouri Baptist Convention's staff reduction in January 2003. She graciously agreed to continue to serve as a volunteer WMU Director through the April 25-26, 2003, Annual Meeting at William Jewell College in Liberty. Debbie Miller said this about Kathy in her President's report in 2003, "We are thankful for the 17 years of ministry provided to Missouri WMU by Kathy Scott."

Kathy began working as Director of Children and Family Ministries at Fee Fee Baptist Church in St. Louis in 2008. She continues to serve there today.

CHAPTER 26

The Leadership of Vivian Hargrove McCaughan

WMU Executive Director

2003-2010

Vivian Gail Hargrove was born on March 6, 1948, to Billy and Imogene Hargrove in Kansas City. She made her profession of faith on December 8, 1957, at Sylvan Hills Baptist Church in Atlanta, Georgia. The missions journey for Vivian began early with involvement in Sunbeams and GAs. She completed all of the GA forward steps to Queen Regent. Her heart for missions was inherited – missions was in her DNA. Her dad, Rev. Billy Hargrove, was a pastor and evangelist. Rev. Hargrove worked in both church surveys and church loans for the Home Mission Board in Atlanta. When the family moved to Jefferson City,

CHAPTER 26

he served on the Missions staff and was Director of the Cooperative Program for the Missouri Baptist Convention. Vivian publicly dedicated her life to Christian service at the age of 12.

In 1962, the family moved to Phoenix, Arizona. Vivian became the pianist and organist at Southern Baptist Temple, where her Dad was pastor. The family moved again in 1965 to Waynesville, Missouri, where Vivian graduated as Valedictorian from Waynesville high school. While in Waynesville, she worked a couple of summers at Windermere Baptist Assembly.

Vivian returned to Phoenix to attend Grand Canyon Baptist College. Using her college days to prepare for her future missions work, she earned a Bachelor of Science degree in elementary education and music. While at Grand Canyon, she spent a summer doing mission work through the Home Mission Board in the Cleveland, Ohio, area.

Her senior year, she applied for the Journeyman program in February of 1969 and was accepted in April before graduation on May 26. Within three weeks, she was in Journeyman training and then was sent to Accra Goodwill Center in Ghana, West Africa, for two years from 1969-1971. Vivian loved her Journeyman experience; she found her place for Christian service in mission work.

Returning from Ghana, Vivian went to Southwestern Seminary in Fort Worth, Texas, in

August 1971 to obtain a Master of Divinity degree. Vivian was a Madge Truex scholarship recipient while at seminary. She did summer missions again in 1972, this time in Youngstown, Ohio. While in Fort Worth, she applied for a foreign missionary appointment with the Foreign Mission Board and was appointed to Togo, West Africa. Vivian graduated from seminary in May of 1974. After a summer of packing and making preparations for living in Africa, Vivian went to the Mission Orientation Center in Callaway Gardens, Georgia. While at the Missions Orientation Center, Vivian met Raymond Hite, a missionary appointee to Hong Kong. They were married and were appointed together to Ghana, West Africa. They served in Kumasi, Ghana, from the summer of 1975 through March 1977, with Vivian doing children's work. They returned to the states in 1977, and the marriage ended in 1982.

Upon returning to the states, Vivian taught in public schools in Crozet, Virginia, and in Jefferson City. While teaching at Callaway Hills Elementary, she started Backyard Bible Clubs in a trailer park in Holts Summit, where many of her students lived. The first summer, she had Backyard Bible Clubs. There were 87 children who came and 27 received Christ. She led Backyard Bible Clubs for twelve years while she taught elementary school. This led her to a lifelong commitment to Multi-Housing ministry. Even though

CHAPTER 26

she couldn't go back to West Africa, Vivian found a mission field in Missouri.

In December 1987, Vivian was appointed by Dr. Larry Lewis of the Home Mission Board to serve as a Multi-Family Housing Consultant for mid-Missouri, based at First Baptist Church in Jefferson City. She began work with the Missouri Baptist Convention in January 1988, when she began her Multi-Housing ministry partnership with MBC. Then she moved to O'Fallon to work with Multi-Housing at Hidden Valley Estates in Wentzville. She saw the 200-unit apartment community as a mission field that could be a place God's love could make a difference in lives where drugs and crime were everyday parts of life. Vivian was also the coordinator of Missouri's World Hunger Fund.

Vivian came to First Baptist Church of St. Clair to speak about Missouri Missions and her work in the Multi-Housing ministry while my husband, Dr. Phil Turner, was pastor. I remember that she told this story about doing a Backyard Bible Club in an apartment complex in the St. Louis area. A little girl came every day to the Bible Club. The little girl's mom was single and worked three jobs, so the little girl was at home alone much of the time. On the last day, the little girl asked Vivian if they would be having this again next week. Vivian said, "No, we won't be having it again next week." The little girl replied, "I like coming to the Backyard Bible Club because every day someone tells me they love me." This story is indicative of how Vivian's life radiated the love of God.

Vivian worked with Curtis and Theresa Smith in North St. Louis County. The Metro North Family Ministry Center served about 450 people each month. While serving as the North American Mission Board's Multi-Housing/Church Planting Missionary, Vivian saw a huge mission field in multi-housing communities. Jim McCaughan, who worked with a St. Louis Associational Youth group, asked Vivian to come and tell them about ministering in the Multi-Housing area close to them. Jim told his youth they could minister in their own community instead of going to another state to do missions. This is where Jim and Vivian met and became acquainted. After having some meetings together, Jim asked Vivian is she would like to go out on a date. Vivian said, "Yes, I would." On April 26, 1997, she married Jim McCaughan, who was the Minister of Missions at Parker Road Baptist Church in Florissant. Vivian and Jim were married for 13 years.

Vivian McCaughan was the Church Planting Strategist, Weekday Ministries Director, and Evangelism Director for the Missouri Baptist Convention. With MBC reorganization in 2000, Vivian was named coordinator for MBC's Missions Mobilization team. In 2003, she served as a Multi-

CHAPTER 26

Housing Church Planting Missionary and Church Multiplication Specialist. Also, that year WMU became part of her responsibilities, and WMU/Women's Ministry Specialist was added to her growing list of titles. In November 2004, the MWMU Board named Vivian McCaughan as Missouri WMU Director. In 2009, Vivian became the team leader of the MBC's Missions and Evangelism Team and served until her death on April 18, 2010. Vivian's focus was meeting and working with people one-on-one. Vivian knew the importance of building relationships first when trying to meet needs. She believed you need to earn the right to share Christ.

In 2007, Vivian was diagnosed with ovarian cancer. After surgery and radiation, she completed two years of chemotherapy. She continued working until 2010, when she took medical leave from her responsibilities as Missouri WMU/Women's Mission and Ministry Specialist and Multi-Housing Church Planting Catalytic Missionary for Missouri Baptist Convention. In March 2010, Vivian and Jim were featured on Day 3 in the Week of Prayer for North American Missions. Vivian had taken medical leave and was unable to attend the April 9-10, 2010, Missions Celebration in St. Joseph.

I was serving as WMU Secretary at the time, and the WMU Board requested that a letter be composed on behalf of the Board members. The following is part of the letter to Vivian.

*"The Missouri WMU Board wants to say a big **THANK YOU** for all your faithful and dedicated service to the Lord through Missouri Woman's Missionary Union and the Missouri Baptist Convention. The women attending M-Counter at St. Joseph, April 9-10, took an offering in your honor. A total of $1,185.00 was given to the Alberta Gilpin Fund to help start new WMU organizations. This will enable the work of Woman's Missionary Union to continue to grow and touch the lives of Missouri Baptists. We also hope that this offering lets you know how much you are loved and appreciated. You are dear to us, and we thank you for your committed service to Missouri WMU. You have been a blessing to many people."*

Laura Wells, Missouri WMU Women on Mission Specialist, said this about Vivian, "Her Godly wisdom and faithful service to the Lord has left a wonderful legacy for so many across Missouri, North America, and overseas. Vivian will be greatly missed."

Vivian passed away at her home on April 18 at the age of 62. At Vivian's memorial service on April 24, 2010, at First Baptist Church in Jefferson City, Wanda Lee, national WMU Executive Director, Birmingham, Alabama, paid tribute to Vivian. Representing

CHAPTER 26

Missouri WMU, I spoke at the memorial service about Vivian's contributions and service to Missouri WMU. I said, "Vivian modeled the WMU Watchword, *'Laborers together with God'* (1 Corinthians 3:9). Vivian led by example in demonstrating a missions lifestyle."

CHAPTER 27

The Presidency of Lorraine Rogers Powers

Missouri WMU President
2004-2009

At the 2004 Annual Meeting at Poplar Bluff, Lorraine Powers was elected WMU President and served until 2009.

Lorraine was born December 8, 1945, in Kansas City to Cecil and Jean Rogers. Her parents and older brother were charter members of Spring Valley Baptist Church (SVBC) in Raytown, Missouri. She grew up in SVBC as her parents were very active in the church and its WMU program. Lorraine received Jesus as her Savior in 1952. She was in Sunbeams, Girls Auxiliary, and Royal Ambassadors. She completed Queen Regent in Service in Forward Steps in GAs. She graduated from Raytown high school and attended William Jewell College (WJC). She received

CHAPTER 27

her Bachelor's Degree in 1967. She was a member of the Ann Hasseltine Young Women's Auxiliary. While at WJC, she served as state YWA President.

She completed her master's studies at the University of Missouri at Kansas City and taught in Raytown public schools until taking early retirement in 1997. She married John Powers in 1974, and together they have a son, Nathan.

Lorraine is a member at First Baptist Church in Blue Springs, where she teaches Sunday School and facilitates a Women on Missions group. Lorraine is a certified NAMB English-as-a-Second Language trainer and leads Basic Workshops in Missouri. Lorraine led Girls in Action and Acteen groups and was part of several mission trips in the United States and abroad. She served in different capacities in Blue River-Kansas City Baptist Association. Lorraine served as Chairman of the national WMU Foundation Board of Directors. She is currently WMU Funds Ambassador on the MWMU board, keeping members informed about the national WMU Foundation.

Lorraine's term as president began after her election at the 2004 MWMU Annual Meeting. On November 13, 2004, about 150 women traveled to Jefferson City to attend a celebration of 17 years of the prayer partnership with Lesotho. The Lift Up Lesotho Prayer Rally was held at Concord Baptist Church, Jefferson City. The Gestring family, missionaries serving in Lesotho, spoke at the rally. There was also a video message from Randy Sprinkle. Randy was a catalyst in forming the partnership between Missouri and Lesotho. It was in the spring of 1987 that MWMU's prayer partnership with the country of Lesotho officially began. As Randy and Nancy Sprinkle prepared to begin a work in this small mountain country in South Africa, they challenged Missouri WMU members to "Lift Up Lesotho" in their prayers.

In April 2005, five GA Retreats with the theme "Christ Followers: Reaching the World" were held. The GAs were able to meet missionaries and learn the steps involved in becoming a missionary from application to commissioning. There were over 1,077 girls and leaders in attendance in five Missouri locations, and at least five professions of faith were made. The girls collected over $3,850 for the International Mission Board.

The 82nd Annual Meeting was held at First Baptist Church, Ellisville, on April 15-16, 2005, with 300 persons registered. This was the first meeting for President Lorraine Powers to preside. The theme was "Celebration of Missions: Christ Followers." The underlying theme for the general sessions was "Project Hope: Poverty." Throughout the meeting, missionary Carolyn Houts shared prayer for the missionaries and their work. Referring to Missouri's continued support for Lesotho, Barbara Popp announced an opportunity for some women to go to Lesotho to do Prayer Walking in early November. Debbie Wohler, NAMB missionary in Lake Tahoe, spoke on her calling and her ministry pilgrimage. She thanked the WMU women for collecting the Campbell Soup labels, which provided three vans for her ministry.

Sherry Kinsey, St. Louis Literacy Consultant, presented some facts and shared about her work. Janet and Dudley, missionaries in Italy, shared some of the challenges they faced on the mission field. Theresa Smith, Metro North Family Ministry Center Director, shared about the needs met by their center through Project Help. Alpha Goombi, NAMB Missionary from Omaha, Nebraska, spoke about missions among Native Americans. Alpha, dressed in an Indian ceremonial outfit, closed the meeting doing the Lord's Prayer in Native American sign language.

The 83rd Annual Meeting met on April 28-29, 2006, at Forest Park Baptist Church in Joplin, Missouri, with over 400 women and men in attendance. The theme was "Mission Footprints: The Impact of a Christ Follower." The first missionary who spoke was Iracema, IMB missionary to Paraguay. She grew up in Brazil and decided to follow Jesus' call to missions at the age of nineteen. Nona Renfrow, retired missionary to Brazil, was at the meeting and had been Iracema's teacher. In 2006, a new recognition was added to our Annual Meeting program and that was to honor a missionary. The 2006 Emeritus Missionary of the year was Nona Renfrow, who served for 31 years in Brazil. Iracema and her husband served fifteen years in Uruguay before going to Paraguay. Randy Poole, NAMB missionary in Tennessee, spoke on his work in the Mississippi River ministry. Larry, missionary to Romania, shared about the great impact of Missouri Baptists in Romania. He related that there are Missouri Baptist "footprints" all over Romania.

Lorraine Powers, Vivian McCaughan, and Kim Knight presented a skit to celebrate 110 years of preschool mission education. Lorraine introduced Bill and Beverly C. and their daughter Robin and husband David S. Both couples served in Kenya. Vivian held a dialogue with the couples and the three grandchildren. This made three generations of a family involved in missions.

GA Retreats in 2006 continued to draw girls and their leaders from across Missouri. The 2006 theme was "Missions Bootcamp." The GA Retreats were held in six different locations in April. Over 1,100 girls and their leaders attended.

Missouri Acteen Activators traveled to Puerto Rico on a mission trip in July 2006. The Acteens helped with Backyard Bible Clubs, youth activities and

CHAPTER 27

did some painting. The Acteens Retreat held November 10-12, 2006, had 500 in attendance.

The 84th Annual Meeting met on the campus of Hannibal-LaGrange College on April 27-28, 2007. The theme was "M-Counter–Live the Call." This was the first joint meeting of WMU and Women's Ministry with over 500 in attendance. Connie Cavanaugh, Women's Speaker and NAMB Missionary from Canada, gave the Bible study in each session. She urged attendees to believe in the God of miracles. She stressed that we don't have to do everything. In order to embrace the call, she challenged attendees to accept themselves and do what God has gifted them and called them to do.

Missionary speakers at this meeting were Diane Combs, a Missouri missionary, who talked about her first term of service in Belarus. She and her husband are returning to serve in Kazakhstan. Shad and Michelle S., missionaries to Niger, West Africa, also spoke. Michelle shared what it felt like to serve as a missionary and asked for prayer for the Fulani people that they would become the ones to spread the Gospel to the people of West Africa. Kaye Miller, national WMU President, told of being a missionary kid living in the "bush" with her family. Later she invited the group to attend the "Live The Joy Of Missions" event to be held in October in Little Rock. Rosa Cruz, WMU President of Puerto Rico, read a letter of greeting from

Nellie Torrado, Executive Director of Puerto Rico and Virgin Islands WMU. The 2007 Emeritus Missionary of the year was Mariam Misner. Mariam retired from the IMB in 1993 after serving 37 years in Indonesia.

Alberta Gilpin and members of her family were present for the 84th Annual Meeting. She shared briefly with attendees and then autographed her biography, *Enduring Love,* which was available for purchase. Barbara Bray, the author of the book, *Enduring Love,* said, "It was good to sit with Alberta and see the love of those who bought her book."

As in 2006, GA Retreats in 2007 were well attended. Approximately 1,300 girls and leaders enjoyed the retreats centered around the theme: "I Am A Jewel." The six locations were almost to their maximum in housing the GAs and their leaders. The following year another weekend for GA Retreats would be added.

BLUME, the national WMU event for teenage girls, was held in Kansas City during July. More than 4,000 girls and leaders participated. Missouri WMU was proud to acknowledge Christy York as a national WMU Acteen Panelist for 2007. Christy is from Berean Baptist Church in Richland, Missouri. Her mother, Janet York, was her Acteen leader.

As part of the Puerto Rico/Virgin Islands partnership, an MWMU team traveled to Puerto Rico in October 2007 to lead in WMU training.

Over three hundred women attended M-Counter at First Baptist Church, Raytown, on April 26-27, 2008. This 85th Annual Meeting was centered around the theme: "Called Missions and Ministry." Debra Berry from the national WMU led the Bible Study in each general session.

Beulah Peoples was the 2008 Emeritus Missionary of the Year. Beulah served 40 years in denominational work. She served from 1984-1997 in the New England area as WMU Director and Church and Community Ministries Director.

Special missionary speakers were Michelle, who talked about Missions in Malawi, Africa, and Philip and Peggy who spoke about their mission work in El Salvador. Bill and Carol Bowers from Missouri, spoke of their IMB work in Durban, South Africa. Norma McMurray from Giving Thanks Ministries in Ohio was a featured speaker during the general session.

GA Retreats were expanded to seven weekends in 2008. Each retreat was well attended with about 1,400 girls and their leaders. The girls and their leaders focused on the theme: "All the World Is A Stage." Eight salvations occurred at the GA retreats and two salvations happened following the retreats.

Children in Action observed Missions Exploration Day in October 2008 in two locations: one at the Pulaski Baptist Association Camp in Waynesville and the other at Grand Oaks Camp in Chillicothe.

Missouri Acteens celebrated the fact that three Missouri Acteens were chosen by national WMU as 2008 Acteens Top Teens. They were Sierra Bollinger, Larissa Petzoldt, and Kati Miinch. A state Acteens retreat was held in November 2008 with the theme "Soar" at Pulaski Baptist Association Camp, Waynesville.

CHAPTER 28

The Presidency of Joan Harms Dotson

Missouri WMU President
2009-2014

Joan Dotson was elected 19th President of Missouri Women's Missionary Union at the 86th Annual Meeting at First Baptist Church in Lebanon, Missouri, and served for five years.

Joan Harms was born July 11, 1940, to John and Gertrude Harms in Newton, Kansas. Joan lived in Augusta, Kansas until she was married to William H. Dotson in 1959. William (Bill) was in the Navy, and this took the couple to Mountain View, California, where Bill was stationed. Joan and Bill were involved with an American Baptist Church in Sunnyvale, California, where they sponsored a Junior High youth group. Joan participated in the American Baptist Women (ABW) organization at the church. Two sons and a daughter were added to their family during which time Bill and Joan were sponsoring a church singles group and then a College and Career group. Joan was the Chaplain for the ABW in the 1970s and was also the Christian Education Director for two years at their church.

The year 1980 brought Bill and Joan to the State of Missouri through Boeing. Living in Missouri gave them the opportunity to become Southern Baptists, which they did by joining the First Baptist Church in O'Fallon. Joan began WMU at FBC, O'Fallon, and carried on that work as long as she was at the church. Bill and Joan were also instrumental in beginning a new church in Lake Saint Louis, Missouri, in 1986. In 1990, Bill and Joan went back to FBC, O'Fallon, where Joan was secretary to Pastor Gary Taylor for five years. Upon retiring, Joan cared for her mother in their home along with two young granddaughters.

After Bill retired in 2002, the opportunity for mission trips to the United Arab Emirates became available. In addition to going there, Bill and Joan have traveled three times to Mali, West Africa, on mission trips and three times on mission trips to Krasnodar in Russia, and also in Mexico, Canada, and Panama. Telling people about Jesus was and is the goal and mission of Joan's life.

At the 86th Annual Meeting of Missouri WMU, the theme was "Called to Love." There were 381

CHAPTER 28

people registered for this meeting at First Baptist Church, Lebanon, on April 17-18, 2009. Wanda Lee, national WMU Executive Director, was the keynote speaker. Elaine Ham, a North American missionary from Atlanta, Georgia, gave her testimony. Linda, former IMB missionary to Bolivia, shared about her call to the mission field. Linda grew up going to Sunbeams, GAs and Acteens. Her mission experiences helped prepare her to be a missionary. Linda told of a time she was driving home after a prayer conference and there was a cow in the middle of the road. She was able to swerve and barely missed it. The next morning when she went outside to get in her car, she noticed the tail of the cow was attached to the front bumper of her car. Missionaries depend on the prayers of people back home. IMB former missionaries to Argentina, South America, for over 25 years, David and Janene Ford shared their experiences on the mission field.

During the Business Session, it was reported that a new position on the WMU Board would be a WMU Resource Specialist. The following officers were elected to serve for the 2009-2010 year: Joan Dotson, President; Cherri Crump, Vice-President; Jan Turner, Secretary; Belinda Hogan, Treasurer. The MWMU Emeritus Missionary for 2009-2010 was Lucy Wagner, career missionary to South Korea. An offering of $2,200.61 was received for the Madge N. Truex Fund. Based on the 2009 ACP Reports, there had been a 5% increase in Missouri WMU enrollment this past year.

During the MWMU Board meeting held on July 17, 2009, at Jefferson City, Teri Broeker reported that she went to Puerto Rico to help with Children's Camp. Vivian Howell is the new Mission Friends Specialist, and this was her first meeting.

In 2009, approximately 1,300 girls and leaders focused on allowing God to make their hearts to be like HIS. The retreats spread over three weekends and eight locations across Missouri.

In the fall of 2009, another annual highlight for MWMU was the Missionary Family Retreat for Emeritus Missionaries who have served with International Mission Board, North American Mission Board, and Missouri Baptist Convention. About fifty emeritus missionaries attended.

The 87th Annual Meeting was held April 9-10, 2010, at Fredrick Boulevard Baptist Church, St. Joseph. Over 300 women attended this meeting; its theme was "Called To Serve." In 2010, the MBC Book of Reports reported there were 19,248 enrolled in WMU, according to the ACP reports turned in by the churches. Joan Dotson, President, had to carry on the meeting without the help of the MWMU Executive Director, Vivian McCaughan, who was on medical leave. Dr. David Tolliver, MBC Executive Director, who was at the meeting, said he didn't see Vivian

CHAPTER 28

being able to return to work. IMB missionaries sharing their testimony at M-Counter were Jackie B., Chile, and May C., Nigeria. Sandra Williams, NAMB missionary from Elkhorn, Kentucky, and Curt & Diana Patty, NAMB missionaries from St. Louis, gave their testimonies. Debbie Taylor Williams, author and speaker from Kerrville, Texas, spoke on the topic of her book, *If God is in Control, Why Am I a Basket Case?*

At the 2010 meeting, there were twenty new WMU age-level organizations started in 17 churches with at least one new start in each age level (3 Mission Friends, 2 Girls in Action, 3 Children in Action, 2 Youth on Mission, and 10 Women on Mission). At least one new organization was started in each of the eight MWMU regions. Eight of these churches representing seven of the regions were present and recognized. Eight churches received a $100 Bidstrup Scholarship for beginning an organization in a church without WMU. The Madge Truex committee named Leona Troop Macklin, retired missionary to Brazil for 35 years, as the 2010 Emeritus Missionary.

Prior to the 2010 Annual Meeting, the MWMU Board of Directors had a meeting with guests Dr. David Tolliver, MBC Executive Director, and Jerry Field, MBC staff. Jerry Field talked to the board about what was going to happen with Vivian's job. For the immediate future, three contract workers would be secured to take over some of Vivian's job responsibilities: one contract worker for Women's Ministry, one contract worker for preschool, children and youth missions work, and one contract worker for the adult/WMU work.

At the September 11, 2010, WMU Council Meeting, members learned that there was a proposal to be voted on at the Missouri Baptist Convention in October to establish the Vivian McCaughan Missional Living Endowment Fund. There is already $790,000 in this Endowment fund. It will be administered through the MBC Foundation. This endowment will be used for multi-housing, church planting, partnership missions, and leadership development. There were also plans to sell the Alberta Gilpin Missionary house. The funds from the sale of the house will go toward the Vivian McCaughan Missional Living Endowment Fund. The missionary house became too expensive to maintain. It was going to need some extensive repairs. There had only been one missionary who stayed in it the last three years. The items in the house (furnished by MWMU and associational WMU) were sold at a garage sale. The money received from the garage sale went to the Madge N. Truex Fund and to the Vivian McCaughan Endowment Fund. Madge N. Truex Fund received $500, and $1,503 went into the Vivian McCaughan Endowment Fund. At the Missouri Baptist

CHAPTER 28

Convention in October, an offering of $4,000 was given for the Vivian McCaughan Endowment Fund, which made the total for the Endowment Fund over $800,000.

The 88th Annual Meeting was held April 15-16, 2011, at First Baptist Church, Springfield. The theme was "Unhindered." There were 438 people registered. A NAMB missionary on the program was Nadeine Gold from Mountain Country Ministries. She worked in resort ministries in the Branson area with over 400 volunteers a year. Alicia Wong, NAMB missionary in Women's Evangelism from Atlanta, gave her testimony. The keynote speaker was Sharon Hoffman, founder of Gifted Living Ministries. She is an author and speaker from Springfield, Missouri. Jason and Dorothea, IMB missionaries to West Africa, shared about their work. Cherri Crump recognized the new starts. Each new start got a button and a gift certificate to the WMU Bookstore. There were a total of 59 new starts: 10 Mission Friends; 9 Girls in Action; 15 Children in Action; 4 Acteens; 6 Youth on Mission; 11 Women on Mission; 4 Adults on Mission. Teri Broeker reported there were 147 in attendance at the 2010 Acteen Retreat. Teri also reported there were 1,205 in attendance at the seven GA Retreats, which represented 95 churches in 2010. Two girls made professions of faith, and one girl committed her life to missions. In 2011, 1,322 girls and leaders were registered for GA Retreats, with twenty new churches attending.

Vicki Brown reported $1,692.65 was collected for the Madge N. Truex Fund. Cherri Crump reported there were 51 gift baskets brought to the Silent Auction, which sold for a total of $1,857.00, which goes to the Alberta Gilpin Fund. The MWMU Emeritus Missionary for 2011-2012 was Beverly Richardson, who served in Jordan as a teacher for 27 years. Julianne gave her missionary testimony. She had served as an IMB missionary journeyman for three years. Julianne was a product of MWMU. She received an Acteen scholarship to attend SBU. She thanked MWMU for the influence they had on her life. As a journeyman, her job was translating Bible stories. She trained the people to tell Bible stories so they could share the stories with others. Norma Tolbert gave the Ministry Project report. There were eight different mission projects going on with 172 participants. There were 35 large boxes of donated items filled and sent to Grand Oak Mission and Convoy of Hope in Green County. There were over 1,100 salvation witnessing bracelets made.

At the April 2011 MWMU board meeting, it was reported there was a total of $947,626.16 in the Vivian McCaughan Endowment Fund, which is being overseen by the Missouri Baptist Foundation.

CHAPTER 28

Applications for the funds will be taken after the endowment reaches the $1 million mark.

During the April 2012 MWMU Board meeting, members were told about the reorganization of the Missouri Baptist Convention, which was approved by the MBC Executive Board. The reorganization resulted in seven teams. Rick Hedger is the team leader for Missional Evangelism and Discipleship. This team includes Evangelism/Prayer & Spiritual Awakening, Partnerships, Disaster Relief, and WMU.

The Missouri WMU 89th Annual Meeting was held April 20-21, 2012, at First Baptist Church, Jackson. The theme was "Live Sent-Unhindered." There were 342 people registered. Bill and Carol Bowers, IMB missionaries to South Africa, explained about Training for Trainers as a way of storying. Bill told about a block party at a Baptist Church which resulted in 50 youth being reached by the church. Other IMB Missionaries who spoke were Gary and Carolyn from Europe. They started an English club for young people. They also held sports camps to try and reach the unsaved young people. Vince Blubaugh, the Missions Pastor at Second Baptist Church, Springfield, gave the theme interpretations during each worship service.

NAMB missionaries speaking at the meeting were George and Cathy Chinn, the Mississippi River Ministry Coordinators. George said his ministry involved trying to find resources and match them up with the needs of the people. George gave the illustration of a farmer who took old bicycles from dumpsters, junkyards, and garage sales and fixed them up. He painted them and took them to impoverished areas, and handed them out to kids who never had a bicycle.

Daniel and Kimberly Goombi, NAMB missionaries for the Native American Reservations in Kansas, spoke at the meeting. Daniel works with the Prairie Band Potawatomi Nation in their Family Violence Prevention Program. Daniel ministers to people who have been abused or sexually assaulted. The ratio is higher than average among Native Americans for abuse and assault. Sharon Fields-McCormick, a Mission Service Corps Missionary with the North American Mission Board, helped establish the Atlanta Pregnancy Resource Center. Sharon works with churches to get involved in addressing the issue of domestic human trafficking and the commercial sexual exploitation of children.

The 2012 Emeritus missionaries were Ron and Ina Winstead. The Winsteads had served for over 25 years in East Asia. The annual Missionary Family Retreat was held at Cross Pointe Retreat Center on Lake of the Ozarks in the fall. There were forty-two participants in attendance.

CHAPTER 28

The Morning Watch on Saturday morning was led by Barbara Popp, past WMU President. The emphasis of the prayer time was celebrating the Missouri WMU Prayer Partnership with Lesotho which began in 1987. Randy and Nancy Sprinkle were the first SBC missionaries to go to the small mountain kingdom within the confines of South Africa. In celebration of the 25th Anniversary of the partnership, women from all over the state made 605 denim bags to fill with school supplies. The Floras, IMB missionaries, will give them to the children in the mountains of Lesotho to encourage them with their education and to use as a witnessing tool. Missouri WMU women have followed the lives of many missionaries who have invested themselves in ministering and witnessing to the Basotho people and have continued to undergird their work with prayer.

National WMU celebrated 125 years as an organization in 2013, and Missouri WMU celebrated this milestone at the 90th Annual Meeting and Missions Celebration at First Baptist Church, Warrensburg, April 12-13, 2013. "The Story Lives On: Celebrate, Connect, Commit" was the theme. Four hundred sixty-eight people registered for the meeting. Debby Akerman, national WMU President, presented the theme interpretation. NAMB missionaries giving their testimonies at this Missions Celebration were Jon and Mindy Jamison. Their work was in the inner city of Des Moines, Iowa, where they served at the Friendship Baptist Center. Ken McClure, NAMB Missionary and MBC Multicultural Church Planting Catalyst, shared his mission in Missouri. Ken said that we can do foreign missions right here in our own state. Over 250,000 people in Missouri were born outside the United States. Over 16,000 college students from other countries or states are in Missouri.

IMB Missionaries speaking during the Missions Celebration were Charles and Bette who shared about their work in Russia; Trevor and Kimberly who serve in West Africa in the Sub-Saharan Africa Affinity Group; and Elizabeth, who ministers to the Japanese people as a church planter.

Carolyn Houts received the 2013 Emeritus Missionary of the year award. Carolyn served for 35 years in Ghana as a music promoter. Approximately 40 emeritus missionaries attended the annual Missionary Retreat held at Cross Pointe Retreat Center on Lake of the Ozarks.

There were 720 in attendance at the GA Retreats in 2013, 293 at the RA Congress, and 280 children/leaders attended Mission Exploration.

The 91st Missions Celebration and Annual Meeting was held on April 4-5, 2014, at Second Baptist Church, Springfield. There were 497 people registered for the meeting. Veda Locke received the 2014 Emeritus Missionary of the Year Award. She and

CHAPTER 28

her husband served in Nigeria for 36 years. Jean Roberson, national WMU Ministry Consultant from Birmingham, gave the theme interpretation during the Worship Celebration. The theme was "The Story Lives On: Celebrate, Connect, Commit." IMB missionary testimonies were given by Charles and Jamie, working in Peru. They have been missionaries for over 26 years. Other IMB missionary testimonies were given by Helmer and Shannon, serving in South Africa. There were 31 new WMU organizations recognized in 2014.

Teri Broeker and her courageous crew oversaw three weekends of GA Retreats in five locations. Seven hundred forty-four girls attended, and 14 professions of faith plus other decisions were made.

CHAPTER 29

The Leadership of Laura Adams Wells

WMU Executive Director
2010-2019

After the passing of Vivian McCaughan in 2010, Laura Wells assumed her duties making her Missouri's tenth WMU Executive Director.

Laura Elizabeth Adams was born on May 7, 1961, in Orange, California, to parents Neil and Charlene Adams. She was raised in California for nine years, then moved to Haines, Alaska. She then moved to Ketchikan, Alaska, and graduated high school there. After high school, she attended Faith Baptist Bible College in Ankeny, Iowa, for one year, then moved to Carstairs, Alberta, Canada, where she attended Olds Community College. After working for an oil company for a few years in Calgary, Alberta, she moved to Des Moines, Iowa, where she worked for an advertising agency.

She then felt the Lord calling her to full-time

CHAPTER 29

ministry. She moved to Kansas City and worked for Gospel Missionary Union as a secretary. Gospel Missionary Union (GMU) was a missionary-sending organization that sent missionaries all over the world. It was while working for GMU that she felt called to be more involved in missions, going wherever the Lord sent her. She attended William Jewell College in Liberty, Missouri, and graduated in May 1992 with a B.A. in Vocal Music Education.

She met her husband, David Wells, at Gashland Baptist Church in Kansas City. They were married at Gashland Baptist Church on December 22, 1989. In 1993, they moved to Lyman, Wyoming, where her husband became pastor at Bridger Valley Baptist Church. While living in Lyman, Wyoming, Laura became involved in Women on Mission and eventually became the church's WMU director. She then went on to serve as Associational WMU Director. A year later, she became Wyoming's WMU Women's Consultant. She served in this position for four years before moving to Missouri in 2003.

After moving to Missouri, she became Missouri WMU's Adult Specialist under Vivian McCaughan's leadership. She served as the Adult Specialist for five years until being hired as the Missouri WMU Executive Director in 2010. She served in this position for nine years until moving to Texas in 2019, where her husband serves with Texas Baptist Men as Disaster Relief Director.

CHAPTER 30

The Presidency of Cherri Hall Crump

Missouri WMU President
2014-2019

Cherri Hall Crump was elected 20th President of Missouri Woman's Missionary Union at the 91st Annual Meeting at Second Baptist Church in Springfield, Missouri, and served for five years.

Cherri Hall was born July 23, 1951, to Herman and Lucile Hall. She was born in Columbia, Missouri, and grew up there with one younger brother. Herman was an engineer and worked for the University of Missouri Agricultural Engineering Extension. Lucile was a homemaker. Her parents were active members of FBC of Columbia and provided a Christian family.

Cherri accepted Jesus Christ as her Savior and was baptized at age nine. Sunbeams, Girl's Auxiliary, and Young Women's Auxiliary were important in her spiritual growth. In 1971, while in college at Missouri University, she married Albert Crump, her high school sweetheart. A son was born while Albert was in law school. They later moved to Rolla, where Albert practices law. A daughter and another son were born in Rolla.

Cherri has volunteered in many community activities, including literacy, and President of the Mental Health Association of Missouri. She was a board member of the Missouri Baptist Children's Home for several terms. She served in her church and association through WMU, Sunday School, and many other positions. She served on the Missouri WMU Board of Directors for sixteen years, from 2003-2019, serving as South Central Regional Consultant, Vice-President, President-Elect, and President for the last five of those years.

During Cherri's term as President, the following Missions Celebrations were held from 2015-2019. The 2015 Missions Celebration was held April 10-11 at First Baptist Church of St. Charles. The theme was "All for You-Surrender-Sacrifice-Serve." Three hundred sixty-six registered for the meeting. Wanda Lee, national WMU Executive Director, gave the theme interpretations during the general sessions. Choices of four breakout sessions with ten or more different topics were offered. Missionary speakers who gave testimonies were Don and Diane C., who spoke about their service in Europe, and R.W., who served with the Sub-Saharan African Peoples. Noah Oldham, NAMB Church-Planting Coordinator, shared about his work with SEND St. Louis. Rob Phillips, Missouri Baptist Convention Communications Team Leader, gave his personal testimony and shared what Christians should know about Islam. The 2015 Emeritus Missionaries were Emmett and LaNell Barnes, who served in Morocco. The Mission Action project during this meeting was packing Buckets of Love. One hundred buckets were packed during the meeting by sixty people. There were 133 packed buckets brought to the meeting. A total of 233 buckets were packed and ready to be sent. These buckets were being prepared to send to Southern Africa to be used with persons affected by HIV/AIDS and other persons to open a door to share the gospel.

In April 2015, four hundred boys and leaders attended RA Congress at the State Fairgrounds in Sedalia. There were 622 children and leaders that attended Missions Exploration.

In October 2015, more than 40 emeritus missionaries attended the Missionary Retreat held at Cross Pointe Retreat Center by the Lake of the Ozarks.

More than 100 teen girls and leaders attended PURSUIT at Baptist Hill in Mount Vernon. Girls heard testimony from Tish Hedger, attended breakout sessions, and participated in ministry projects in the community.

Later in 2015, at the November 13-14 MWMU Board meeting, it was reported that Missouri Baptists had sent 804 buckets for the Buckets of Love Project. Seventeen thousand dollars was donated for this project.

The 93rd Annual Meeting and Missions Celebration was held April 8-9, 2016, at Midwestern Baptist Theological Seminary in Kansas City. The theme was "All for You-Surrender-Sacrifice-Serve." There were 325 registered for the meeting, with 280 being WMU members. The Emeritus Missionaries for 2016 were Joe and Carol Barbour. They served in Zambia for ten years. Rosalie Hunt, author, speaker, retired IMB missionary, and former national WMU Recording Secretary, gave the theme interpretations during the worship sessions. Matthew and Angela Swain, music professors at Midwestern Baptist Theological Seminary, led the worship music.

Missionary testimonies were given by Jared and Michelle from South Asia. They are a product of WMU, being involved in RAs and GAs as children. Darrel and Kimberly, IMB missionaries with European Peoples, shared about their ministry. Matt Marrs, NAMB SEND Kansas City missionary, shared about the influence of WMU in the different stages of his life. Carol Bowers, MWMU Prayer Advocate, gave a report on behalf of Baptist Global Response. She thanked everyone for participating in the Buckets of Love Project. A grand total of 2,447 buckets were donated during the collection period.

Teri Broeker reported the Missions Exploration held in October had 622 in attendance in five locations around the state. There were 500 girls and leaders who attended five GA Retreats in October. More than 400 were in attendance at the 2016 RA Congress in Sedalia. Laura Wells reported several new WMU organizations were started in 2016.

Missouri WMU helped host the national WMU Missions Celebration and meeting in St. Louis in June 2016. It was a farewell to national WMU Executive Director Wanda Lee, who was retiring. In July, Sandy Wisdom-Martin became the new national WMU Executive Director.

The Missionary Retreat for retired Missouri missionaries was held in October with a theme of "Vessels for the Master's Use." Thirty-six missionaries attended the retreat at Cross Point on Lake of the Ozarks.

The 2017 Missions Celebration and 94th Annual Meeting occurred April 7-8 at First Baptist Church in Lebanon. The theme was "By All Means." There were 315 people registered with 232 WMU members attending. Linda Cooper, national WMU President, presented the theme interpretations during the worship services. Two IMB missionary families from

CHAPTER 30

Southeast Asian Peoples and South Asian Peoples shared about their work in Indonesia and India. The missionaries focused on training national believers to share the gospel, disciple new believers, and start new churches. (Names omitted for security reasons). Carl and Martha Rees were selected as the 2017 Emeritus Missionaries. They served in Middle America, Honduras and Mexico from 1978-2006. Twenty-eight WMU organizations were recognized as New Starts in 2017.

The 2018 Missions Celebration and the 95th Annual Meeting was held April 6-7 at South Gate Baptist Church in Springfield. There were 328 registered with 241 being members of MWMU. The theme was "By All Means." Kristy Carr, national WMU, Affinity Networks Manager & Senior Manager, interpreted the theme. Harold Cummins was the 2018-2019 Emeritus Missionary. Harold and his wife Betty served as missionaries mainly in Kenya for 33 years. Missionary testimonies were given by Aaron and Melissa, serving the Northern African and Middle Eastern Peoples. They shared stories about how they were called to the ministry. Other IMB Missionaries, Brian and Sheena, shared stories of how God was moving and working in their country. Dr. John Yeats, Executive Director of Missouri Baptist Convention, said the Missouri Missions Offering exceeded the goal of $710,000. The 2017 offering amount was $759,920. Dr. Yeats presented Laura Wells, MWMU Executive

Director/Consultant, a check for $4,920 to use for MWMU work.

Twenty-five new WMU organizations in 19 churches were started in 2018 and were recognized. The new starts represented all age levels of preschool, children, students, and adults. Forty-five people participated in several different mission projects while at the Missions Celebration. An offering of $2,199.00 was collected for the Madge Truex Fund.

In 2018, 303 girls in grades 1-6 and their leaders attended the GA Retreats in October. Five decisions were made for salvation. The RA Congress was held in April 2019 at Sedalia. Eight regional training events were offered across the state with over 350 in attendance.

During the Annual Meeting on Saturday morning, the following officers were elected: President, Cherri Crump; President-Elect, Mary Ann Randall; Vice-President, Connie Craig; Secretary, Jewellene Shortell; Treasurer, Sandi Malone.

The 2019 Missions Celebration and the 96th Annual Meeting was held at First Baptist Church, Kearney, on April 5-6. The theme was "Unshakable Pursuit." There were 235 in attendance. Rosalie Hunt, an author, former IMB missionary, and past national WMU recording secretary, challenged attendees to pursue God without wavering. This Annual Meeting was the last one for Laura Wells, MWMU's Executive

CHAPTER 30

Director/Consultant. She held this position for nine years and resigned to move with her husband, David, who was joining the staff of the Texas Baptist Convention. Mariam Misner was honored as the 2019-2020 Emeritus Missionary. Mariam was a Registered Medical Technologist. The Missouri WMU Madge Truex Fund gave her a scholarship for her seminary training at the Carver School of Missions. Mariam served in Indonesia as a medical lab technician and teacher for 37 years.

Several IMB missionaries shared testimonies at this Missions Celebration, including Tim and Becky, who work with American People in Mexico. Jim and Teresa, IMB missionaries in Lesotho since 2009, told about their work as church planters. Julie shared about her work as a team strategy leader with people groups in North Africa. Michael Porter, NAMB Church Planting Assessor and Coach in Parkville, Missouri, told how his church had baptized over 125 people in twelve years.

Dr. John Yeats, Executive Director of the Missouri Baptist Convention, reported the Missouri Mission Offering was 30% higher than the previous year. He presented a check for $8,110.43 to Missouri WMU.

CHAPTER 31

The Leadership of Bonnie Hildreth Carter

WMU Executive Director
2019-2021

Bonnie Carter was the eleventh WMU Executive Director of Missouri. Bonnie assumed duties with Missouri WMU on June 1, 2019, after Laura Wells moved to Texas.

Bonnie Hildreth was born in New Haven, Connecticut, on June 2, 1962, to Marshall and Mary Hildreth. She was raised in both Connecticut and Michigan. Bonnie accepted Jesus as her Lord and Savior at Wick Road Baptist Church in Taylor, Michigan, during a Mission Event. Soon after that, Bonnie felt God calling her into ministry with missions being a central focus. She graduated from J.F. Kennedy high school in Taylor, Michigan, in 1981.

CHAPTER 31

After moving to Florida, Bonnie attended The Baptist College of Florida from 1984-1989 and received her Bachelor of Arts in Religious Education with a focus on Missions and Students. While at college, Bonnie was introduced to WMU by Jaqueline Draughon and became part of a BYW group on campus. This is where she fell in love with WMU and its importance. She also became a GA and Acteen leader at her church. While in college, she met and married her husband, Mark Jeffrey Carter, on May 23, 1987. After graduating from college, Bonnie and Mark had their first child, Kayla, August 28, 1989, and 13 months later, their second daughter, Alicia, was born on October 17,1990. By this time, Mark was attending Southeastern Baptist Theological Seminary in Wake Forest, North Carolina.

While in North Carolina, Bonnie led GAs at the church where Mark was part-time music minister. She was also active in the church's WMU adult group. One of her favorite things at the church was writing and performing monologues of the great ladies in WMU, including Lottie Moon, Annie Armstrong, and Fannie Heck.

The Carter family moved to Palatka, Florida, in 1993 when Mark became the Minister of Music/Youth at College Park Baptist Church. Bonnie continued to be active in Baptist Women and led GAs. Her family's love for missions grew, and they started a Mission focus drama ministry with students. In 1996, they went with the SBC to the Summer Olympics with their drama ministry.

After moving to Missouri in 1997, Bonnie continued to help with Acteens and Women on Mission at First Baptist Church of Paris. Their family was blessed when their son, Jeromy, was born on March 13, 2002. All Bonnie's children participated in GAs, Acteens, and RAs while growing up.

In 2006, Bonnie developed Crossroads Baptist Association Student Mission Team, which allowed high school students to be on mission in the association as well as in multiple states and Canada. She went on mission trips to Belarus, Russia, Wisconsin, Maine, Minnesota, Montana, Colorado, Nebraska, Wyoming, and Canada. She was a Mission Service Corp Missionary for the North American Mission Board from 2006-2012.

Bonnie became involved in Missouri WMU by helping with GA retreats and Acteen Conferences which led to her becoming a Student Special Worker and then Student Specialist.

In 2008, their two daughters, Kayla and Alicia, died in a car accident. In that year, Bonnie and Mark started a new ministry at Carpenter Street Baptist Church at Moberly in music and youth. While at Carpenter Street Baptist Church, Bonnie remained active in Women On Mission and led Acteens for

CHAPTER 31

many years.

Bonnie was selected as MWMU's Executive Director on June 1, 2019, and served until July 2021. She helped lead MWMU in a time of transition, and her focus was on promoting missions, the Mission Offerings, and WMU. Her goal was for MWMU to partner with Missouri Baptist Churches to be on mission where they were and beyond. She was always looking for ways MWMU could help the local church. She worked to find ways to engage WMU groups with missionaries and Church Planters.

CHAPTER 32

The Presidency of Mary Ann Collier Randall

Missouri WMU President
4/2019-11/2019

Mary Ann Randall was elected 21st President of Missouri Woman's Missionary Union at the 96th Annual Meeting at First Baptist Church in Kearney April 6, 2019, and served for seven months.

Mary Ann Collier was born on January 5, 1963. Her parents, Joe and Ruth Collier, were members of Park Hill Baptist Church in Parkville, Missouri. She still has the pink New Testament given to her from the Park Hill Baptist WMU as a gift at her baby dedication service. Joe and Ruth were involved in promoting missions as well as being a part of a church plant team, which started a church in Waldron, Missouri, in 1971. Mary Ann was eight when this church was started. This was the same year she accepted Christ as her Lord and Savior. She remembers this time vividly, as her family established lifelong friendships with many of the people they met in Waldron. She was a GA at Park Hill and later an Acteen member when her family became part of Harmony Heights Baptist Church.

Mary Ann moved to Arlington, Texas, to attend college. It was while attending Meadow Lane Baptist Church that she knew that God was calling her to pursue a mission lifestyle. Her parents were living in Lebanon at that time, and she returned to that area to see what direction God would lead.

In April 1986, she married Mark Randall. Their daughter, Shea, was born in 1989. They have been active at Hillcrest Baptist Church in Lebanon for nearly 35 years. Mary Ann led GAs and was part of the Baptist Young Women group in her early years there. She continues as a member of Baptist Women, now called Women on Mission.

In 2009, God brought her to realize that He was preparing her for a new mission. One year later, she and a friend were given an opportunity to go to West Africa and learn about sharing stories from God's Word with those who did not have access to the Bible. Upon arrival, she felt as though she had "come home." God has continued to allow her to be part of sharing in West Africa, and she has participated in 16 mission trips there in ten years.

Mary Ann served as Associational WMU Director and was Missouri WMU Secretary from 2014-2018.

CHAPTER 33

The Presidency of Connie Meeker Craig

Missouri WMU President
11/2019-4/2020

Connie Craig assumed the presidency of MWMU in November 2019. She served in that position until April 2020, the shortest Presidential term in MWMU history.

Connie was born on June 8, 1945, to Dale and Frances Meeker in a small rural town of Eldora in central Iowa. Connie attended K-12 grades in the Eldora School system. Connie made a profession of faith at the age of 8 and was baptized at 14 years of age. She graduated high school in 1963. After high school, Connie attended Northeast Missouri State University (now Truman University) in Kirksville and graduated in 1968 with a degree in Music Education.

CHAPTER 33

Connie married Lt. Larry Craig in 1971, and she enjoyed (for the most part) a 25-year, all-expense paid tour of the United States via the US Army with God-designed assignment locations. Connie and Larry have two outstanding children and five of the greatest grandkids ever.

Her WMU experience began in 1974 in California, where she was involved in launching a Baptist Young Women's group in her church and leading a Missions Friends group. Following that start, she has led mission groups in all age levels in associations and local churches and was on state leadership teams from California to Kansas, to Minnesota, to Alaska, to Virginia, and to Missouri.

Since moving to Missouri in 1993, Connie has served MWMU as Adult Special Worker and Regional Consultant in the Northeast region; she also served as Adult Specialist and Vice-President for MWMU. She currently serves as WMU Director for Bethel Baptist Association and in her local church in Hannibal. In each leadership opportunity, there have been outstanding missions-minded women who have guided and encouraged her to bring missions to the forefront in the lives of men, women, and children.

Because of the Covid-19 pandemic, the 2020 Missions Celebration, RA Congress, and Girls Experiencing Missions (G.E.M.) were canceled. Churches as well as WMU groups had to look for new methods of having meetings. Zoom became the means to have virtual meetings via the internet for schools, churches, and WMU.

The World Health Organization declared the outbreak of the coronavirus disease (COVID-19) a public health emergency. The disease is caused by severe acute respiratory syndrome. The virus spread rapidly worldwide. The pandemic had caused more than 589 million cases worldwide and resulted in over six million deaths, making it one of the deadliest pandemics in history. In Missouri, over 1.6 million cases were reported, which resulted in over 21,000 deaths. Hospitals were filled to capacity with patients having Covid. This pandemic caused churches to close, schools to close, and restaurants were closed. People were advised to stay at home.

Because of the pandemic, national WMU had to think creatively on how to continue missions' discipleship in the churches. Downloadable materials were made available for mission leaders to use. Missouri WMU used zoom calls and Facebook to pass along missions information.

CHAPTER 34

The Presidency of Jan Currence Turner

Missouri WMU President
4/2020 - present

Janice Currence was born on January 17, 1950, in Eldon, Missouri, to Jerald and Betty Currence. Jerald was a farmer, and Betty worked as a bookkeeper. Jan grew up at First Baptist Church, Eldon. Jan's mom was the church pianist and organist for over 50 years at First Baptist Church, Eldon. Jan has been involved in WMU since attending Sunbeams as a preschooler. Missions has become a part of her life. She sees WMU as a way she can serve the Lord by praying for our missionaries, by giving to the mission offerings, and by participating in a variety of mission projects.

As a young child, she participated in a Queen coronation at church by wearing a white dress and carrying a crown on a pillow for one of the Queen candidates. Two of the young women who were crowned as queens went on to become foreign missionaries. Jan became exposed to missions at a young age since her mom was involved in Baptist Women and was the WMU Director at First Baptist Church for many years.

Jan made her profession of faith at the age of nine and was baptized at the First Baptist Church of Eldon. When Jan was in grade school, she was active in Girls Auxiliary and worked on the Forward Steps. Her goal was to be a Queen, and she succeeded in achieving that goal. The GA Coronations in the 1960s were big deals. The Queen candidates wore long white formals and had to recite part of the Forward Steps work that had been accomplished. One of the things Jan remembered studying was the life of Esther. One of the highlights of her summers was going to GA Camps at Lake of the Ozarks, hearing the missionaries, and enjoying the activities. Some of her best friends were members of Girls Auxiliary.

After graduation from Eldon High School, Jan attended Southwest Baptist College in Bolivar and was very happy to discover they had an active Baptist Young Women's (BYWs) organization. A dear little lady, affectionately known as Hazel (Mom) Craig, was one of the BYW sponsors. As a freshman, Jan got involved in meeting with one of the BYW groups. Jan

CHAPTER 34

was active in BYWs all four years of college. Between her junior and senior year of college, she felt God calling her to be a summer missionary while attending a Baptist Student Union Convention. She served that summer outside of Chicago, Illinois, as a summer missionary with the Home Mission Board. After that summer, she felt God calling her to full-time Christian Service. During her senior year, she was elected President of the College Baptist Young Women's organization at Southwest Baptist. There were over 200 members of the BYWs with ten different groups.

At the BYW spring banquet in March 1973, Alberta Gilpin was the guest speaker. She was the State BYW Director at that time. She told Jan about the state WMU Annual Meeting that was going to take place in April 1973 at Poplar Bluff, where they would celebrate the 50th Anniversary of Missouri WMU. Since it was on a weekend, Jan attended her first WMU state meeting. Jan was inspired by the meeting and the speakers.

After Jan graduated from college in 1973, she worked the following summer with the Sunday School Board at Ridgecrest Baptist Conference Center in North Carolina. She had made plans to attend Southwestern Theological Seminary, Fort Worth, Texas, in September. In August, Jan received a call from Alberta Gilpin from the Missouri Baptist Convention in Jefferson City. Alberta told Jan that she was the new WMU Executive Director since Mary Bidstrup had retired. Alberta needed someone to be the Baptist Young Women's Director and asked Jan if she would be interested in flying back to Missouri for an interview. Jan met with Alberta Gilpin, Barbara Bray, Viola Scherff, and Marilyn Coble, who formed the personnel committee. In August 1973, Jan was hired as a state missionary serving as the Missouri Baptist Young Women's Director.

Jan thought she had the best WMU mentor in Missouri with Alberta Gilpin as her boss and friend. WMU was the way she could serve in ministry and fulfill her calling to full-time Christian Service. Jan served as Baptist Young Women's Director from 1973-1977. During this time, she led Baptist Young Women and Baptist Women conferences in Missouri, Colorado, Texas, Glorieta Baptist Conference Center in New Mexico, and Ridgecrest Baptist Conference Center in North Carolina. Jan organized and was in charge of WMU bus trips to New Mexico, North Carolina, and Washington, D.C. Jan said, "The MWMU staff was more like extended family. The years I worked for Missouri WMU were some of my busiest yet most fulfilling years in ministry."

"One thing that sticks out in my mind," remarks Jan Turner, "was the prayer meetings that followed our weekly staff meetings. Alberta was a dedicated prayer warrior. If I had difficulties or a problem, I

CHAPTER 34

always felt I could go to Alberta and ask her to pray with me. She was also a wise counselor. One day I walked into her office and asked, 'How do you know who you should marry?' Alberta told me, 'The right man.'" I then told her that I felt God calling me to become a pastor's wife.

I resigned my position to marry Rev. Phil Turner. It was a bittersweet time because I had enjoyed the last four years of ministry. We were married on March 12, 1977, with the WMU staff being part of the wedding party. Alberta offered wise marriage counseling as we have now been married for over 46 years.

After Jan was married, her WMU experience switched from the state level to local church and associational leadership, being WMU Director, Baptist Women Director, and Women on Mission Coordinator through the years. Jan and Phil became parents to their daughters: Joanna in 1986 and Sarah in 1990. Joanna married Aaron Decker in 2006. Joanna and Aaron have three sons: Joseph, Jaxon, and Jonas. Aaron serves as Worship Pastor at First Baptist Church in Neosho. Joanna graduated from Missouri Southern with a degree in Accounting and works as a Financial Analyst. Sarah graduated from Missouri Baptist University with a degree in Worship Arts. Sarah is serving as a Worship Director and Visual Media Specialist in St. Louis.

Jan served as an MWMU special adult worker for over 20 years after she was married. On the Missouri WMU Board, she held five different positions: Public Relations Director, Communications Consultant, Secretary, President-elect, and President. She was also a Resource Consultant for MWMU and a Missouri Star Team member. The purpose of the Star Teams was to help start new WMU organizations. A highlight of Jan's WMU experiences was being able to attend the 100th Anniversary of the national WMU in May 1988 in Richmond, Virginia. She has been attending WMU Mission Celebrations/Annual Meetings since 1973. Jan has calculated she has been a member of Missouri WMU organizations from preschool to Adult for about 68 years.

Jan served as President-Elect in 2019 when Mary Ann Randall announced she was not going to serve a second term. When Mary Ann resigned her position at the November 2019 meeting, according to the Bylaws, Vice-President Connie Craig became President for five months.

Bonnie Carter, WMU Executive Director, polled the WMU members who had registered online for the Missions Celebration and asked them to vote on the officers so they could assume their duties. This was because of having to cancel the 2020 Mission Celebration. Jan Turner assumed the duties of President at the end of April 2020.

CHAPTER 34

Bill and Carol Bowers were selected to be the 2020 Emeritus Missionaries. They were honored at the June 26, 2020, WMU Board Meeting in Jefferson City.

The WMU Emphasis for 2020-2022 was "Relentless." These two years, WMU challenged its members to be relentless in living authentic faith in Christ, seeking God in prayer, giving sacrificially, and witnessing to others. The watchword for this emphasis was Hebrews 10:39, *But we do not belong to those who shrink back and are destroyed, but to those who have faith and are saved.* This verse encourages believers to be relentless in representing Christ even in the most difficult times.

The year of 2020 was one of those difficult times with most MWMU organizations not being able to meet because of the Covid-19 pandemic. The 2020 annual Missions Celebration was canceled because of the Covid pandemic and the stay-at-home order. Most of the Regional Equip meetings were also canceled as well as RA Congress, children and teens events, and the Missionary Retreat. But regardless of the difficulties, MWMU saw God move in amazing ways. Missions' discipleship continued in 2020 for children and teens through Facebook meetings developed by national WMU. MWMU focused on sharing the love of Jesus to those in their communities, state, nation, and world.

In partnership with the MBC Campus Missionaries and Midwestern Seminary, Spurgeon College, Fusion program, MWMU board members sponsored Jeromy Carter, a student preparing to go to the mission field. MWMU promotes praying for missionaries through the monthly prayer guide, *Missouri PrayerWays*. It is available for individuals, churches, and associations to pray for IMB and NAMB missionaries with Missouri ties, church planters, Directors of Missions, and retired missionaries. The *PrayerWays* can be accessed through an email list, the MWMU webpage, regular mail, and the MWMU Facebook page.

In September 2020, the WMU Council met via zoom. The meeting included speakers on "How to Be an Associational WMU Director," information about Mexico, International Mission Study emphasis, and reports about missionaries who were relentless. In September, MWMU groups promoted the Missouri Missions Offering. The goal for 2020 was $725,000. The total received for the Missouri Missions Offering was $736,628.00.

In October, several MWMU board members attended the Missouri Baptist Convention in St. Charles and worked at the WMU booth. Packets were given to people who came by, and they also received a free book. In a report to the MBC, Jan shared what WMUs were doing in churches around the state.

CHAPTER 34

At the November WMU Board meeting, Teri Broeker, the Preschool/ Children/Student Consultant for eleven years, was honored. Teri decided it was time for her to retire. In addition, Dr. John Yeats shared the Missouri Mission Offering was above the goal and presented MWMU a check for $10,600.

The MWMU Board accepted the challenge from Sandy Wisdom-Martin in 2020 to write to churches in Missouri who had not given to the Lottie Moon Christmas offering in the last three years. About 50% of Missouri churches had not given to this offering. The Missouri Lottie Moon Christmas Offering Goal for 2020 was $4,000,000. Members of the MWMU took this challenge and wrote letters to over 700 Missouri churches. The total received in Missouri for the Lottie Moon Christmas Offering was $4,009,755.67.

On January 12, 2021, MWMU had its first statewide zoom call, "Share the Love for Missions," to help raise money for the Alberta Gilpin Fund. This event included a testimony from Alberta Gilpin, a testimony from Missionary Elizabeth Grace, a short message by Dr. Neil Franks, President of Missouri Baptist Foundation, and a mission work report by Rick Hedger, Multiplying Churches Director, MBC.

In April, MWMU promoted giving to the Annie Armstrong Easter Offering. The goal for Missouri was $2,000,000. The total received was $2,019,944.81.

Again, the Missouri Annie Armstrong Easter offering goal was exceeded!

Missouri RA Congress was successfully held on April 23-24, 2021. There were ninety-three boys registered with more than fifty adult leaders and fifty-six volunteers. Between the Missions Run and the missions offering taken, $448.00 was raised for missions.

The 2021 Missions Celebration was held in September 10-11 at First Baptist Church, Lake St. Louis. At that meeting, Denise Rhoades from Oasis International shared about their ministry with refugees from Afghanistan. As a result of hearing about this ministry and the need for helping refugees, Missouri WMU applied for a Heart Grant from the WMU Foundation and received $5,000 to give to Oasis International Ministry.

At the 2021 Missions Celebration, the Basket Auction had 32 baskets donated. From those baskets, a total of $2,526 was received for the Alberta Gilpin Fund. An offering was taken at the Friday evening session for the Madge Truex Fund, and $2,710 was received. A new way to give to the Madge Truex Fund has been set up online. You may donate to this fund at https://tithe.ly/pledge/#/campaign/3819382.

The Mission Project participants at the 2021 Missions Celebration made 115 study kits for college students, 93 hygiene kits for human trafficking

CHAPTER 34

victims at the Missouri Baptist Children's Home, and 101 local teachers were given a Gideon Bible with a kit and note.

At this 2021 WMU Missions Celebration, 12 new WMU organizations which started over the last two years in the midst of Covid were recognized. A new "Let's Grow" position was added to the board in September. The Let's Grow Consultant, Sharon Paris, will help promote the growth of new WMU organizations. Jan Turner wants Missouri WMU to be intentional about starting new WMU organizations in the state.

In September 2021, MWMU promoted giving to the MMO Offering. The goal for 2021 was $725,000. The total received was $824,446. In December 2021, MWMU promoted the LMCO offering. The Missouri Lottie Moon Christmas Offering goal for 2021 was $4,000,000. A total of $4,154,582 was received.

At the 2021 Missouri Baptist Convention held in Branson, WMU was mentioned in other reports. Paul Chitwood, from the IMB, was very complimentary of WMU and said, "the IMB isn't the IMB without the WMU." Another report from the Baptist Home also mentioned WMU. Cheryl Stahlman said, "I have never seen the high view of WMU at our state level that we have now."

At the beginning of 2022, Cheryl Stahlman became the Missouri WMU Executive Director/

Consultant. Other MWMU Staff include Sarah Schmitt as MyMission/Student Mission Consultant, Abigail Moore as the Children Mission Consultant, Travis Webb as RA/Challengers Consultant, Valerie Howe as Adult Consultant, and Vivian Howell as Preschool Consultant.

The 2022 Missions Celebration and MWMU Annual Meeting was held on April 1-2, 2022, at Concord Baptist Church in Jefferson City. The theme was "Being Relentless." There was a total attendance of 163 participants. Connie Dixon, national WMU President, presented the theme interpretations during the worship services. The 2022 Emeritus Missionaries were Phil and Oretha Brewster, who served as church planters in the Philippines from 1976 to 2006. A total of 25 WMU new starts were recognized. There were new WMU organizations in each of the eight regions.

Michael and Traci Byrd, NAMB Church Planters, shared about their ministry in north St. Louis. The Byrds minister in a very low-income area where about 70% are single-parent homes. IMB Missionaries to Israel shared about their work with youth ministry and youth camps.

Carol Bowers, a former MWMU Board member, shared her WMU story. She grew up going to Sunbeams at First Baptist Church of Lincoln, Missouri. She attended Girl's Auxiliary and achieved

CHAPTER 34

the level of Queen in the Forward Steps program. Carol first felt called to missions at GAs. Carol and her husband Bill were called to the international mission field to serve in Romania. Then they were assigned to South Africa. They served for 15 years overseas. Carol thanked WMU for praying for them. Carol said, "Prayers were definitely felt."

The Alberta Gilpin Basket Auction raised $2,526. The offering for the Madge Truex Fund was $2,710. Dr. Rick Hedger presented a check to Missouri WMU for $9,944.64, which is 10% of the MMO offering, which exceeded the Missouri Missions Offering goal.

During the business session, Cherri Crump, Nominating Committee Chairman, introduced the committee composed of the regional consultants and two members-at-large. The following slate of candidates were presented: Jan Turner, President; Janet York, Vice-President; Juliana Rhea, Secretary; Paula Hupe, Treasurer; Angelia Carpenter, Communications Consultant; Darlene Scott, West Central Region Consultant; Dawn Rost, East Central Region Consultant; Connie Craig, Nominating Committee Chair; Kathy Blevins and Jeannie Campbell, Members-at-Large. The candidates were elected without opposition.

Eight different mission projects took place during the Missions Celebration. There were 30 Beauty Bags Packed for Captive Grace (ministry to exploited women); 200 folders collated for Deaf Camp; 125 witnessing bracelets assembled for the MO State Fair; 14 boxes of hair products and supplies for Faith Maternity; 104 personal cards written to residents at The Baptist Homes; 10 boxes of hygiene supplies for Compass Health; 81 men's hygiene packets and 149 women's hygiene packets prepared for Missouri Disaster Relief; 362 pairs of glasses and 194 eyeglass cases collected.

On September 9-10, 2022, ten Missouri WMU staff and WMU board members traveled to the Montana Southern Baptist Women MPower event. Missouri Baptist Convention partners with the Montana Baptist Convention. During the two-day event, the Missouri board members and staff shared mission action ideas, led sessions to train age-level leaders, provided resource information, and made available WMU resources in a bookstore.

Missouri WMU Executive Director Cheryl Stahlman, and Montana Executive Director Tami Park, signed a covenant to partner with each other to further mission organizations' involvement and discipleship. This partnership covenant was the first of its kind in the history of Missouri WMU. After the document signing, Tami Park presented cutting boards engraved with the outlines of Montana and Missouri to commemorate the event. This partnership agreement will continue until the Missouri Baptist

CHAPTER 34

Convention's partnership with the Montana Southern Baptist Convention concludes.

There was a total of 13 Missouri Baptists who attended the MPower event in Montana. The Missouri Team members are pictured below in front of the Missouri and Montana state flags.

Left to Right: The Missouri Team included Travis Webb, RA/Challengers Consultant; Darlene Scott, West Central Regional Consultant; Beverly Hilton, Northwest Regional Consultant; Cheryl Stahlman, MWMU Executive Director; Sarah Schmitt, My Mission/Student Missions Consultant; Jan Turner, MWMU President; Janet York, MWMU Vice-President; Abigail Moore, GA/Children's Missions Consultant; Joan Dotson, Resource Consultant, Vivian Howell, Preschool Missions Consultant, Bill Dotson, Sandee Hedger, Rick Hedger, Multiplying Churches Director, Missouri Baptist Convention.

CHAPTER 35

The Leadership of Cheryl Marler Stahlman

WMU Executive Director
7/2021- present

Cheryl Marler was born December 8, 1983, in St. Louis to James and Joyce Marler, who divorced before her birth. She was raised through most of her childhood in Gerald, Missouri, with parents Emmett and Joyce Bacon, after living a short time in St. Clair. She grew up attending St. Paul's United Church of Christ in Gerald. She was very active in her church, attending regularly, completing confirmation classes, and was baptized according to the church's traditions. She lived her life until age 15, believing that as long as she believed in God, she would go to heaven. From 2nd grade until she was 19 years old, she attended a UCC church camp, where she heard the true gospel at age

CHAPTER 35

15 and gave her life to Christ. Without discipleship, she fell away from following Christ. At age 19, she married her high-school sweetheart, David Stahlman, Jr.

Two years later, when Cheryl was 21 years old, she and her husband rededicated their lives to Christ at Prospect Baptist Church in Lonedell, Missouri. They had their first child, Mia, on November 10, 2005. Cheryl was active in teaching youth Sunday School class, assisting her husband in leading the youth group, and leading music at Prospect Baptist Church. They had their second child, Hannah, on August 31, 2007. David was called to preach at Duly Baptist Church in St. Clair. They and their two small children began a ministry there where she gained experience in leading VBS, teaching Sunday school, and many, many other tasks in assisting her husband in his ministry. While at Duly, they had their third child, Matthew, on November 24, 2009. After a couple of years, God moved their family to Leslie Baptist Church for David to be Associate/Youth Pastor. Cheryl taught Sunday school, helped plan VBS, and participated in her first mission trip to Gary, Indiana, to pack gospels and New Testaments for World Missionary Press. This trip was the beginning of her desire to get the gospel to others. They had their fourth child, Noah, on July 22, 2011. In 2012, God moved their family again to Memorial Baptist Church in New Haven, Missouri, where they served for five years. She participated in Awana, women's ministry, and local outreach opportunities at Memorial Baptist Church.

Cheryl was introduced to Woman's Missionary Union through her friendship with Valerie Howe, MWMU Adult Specialist. She was brought in as a special worker. A few short years later, she was added to the staff of the Missouri Baptist Convention as the MyMission Consultant. This was a brand-new position to reach young women with a passion for missions. She was able to connect Missouri WMU with collegiate missionaries around the state with support of different kinds. During this time, she served alongside Bonnie Carter, then MWMU Executive Director, who mentored her and grew her excitement for missions' education.

In July 2021, she became the MWMU Executive Director/Consultant. Her passion is to bridge Missouri WMU with young women across the state, igniting a passion to learn about missions, give to missions, pray for missions, do missions, and share the gospel of Christ.

CHAPTER 36

Lesotho-Missouri Prayer Partnership

I am also adding a chapter dedicated to Lesotho and the story of how the partnership with Missouri began. This was a historical event because it was the first time a state had partnered with a new country opened by the Foreign Mission Board.

In the summer of 1986, Randy and Nancy Sprinkle were in Fort Worth, Texas, where Randy was doing post-graduate work in missions and cross-cultural studies at Southwestern Baptist Theological Seminary. The Sprinkles had finished a term of service in Botswana. They received a phone call from Dr. Davis Saunders, area director at the time for all Southern Baptist missions in eastern and southern Africa. He told them there was an opening in a new country of his region where Southern Baptists had not had mission work. The country of Mozambique was being opened to missionaries by its government. When praying Dr. Saunders had been seeking direction regarding who God wanted to send to establish the new Mission. Dr. Saunders was led to call the Sprinkles.

The Sprinkles began to pray early each day for God's direction of where their next mission field would be located. As the Sprinkles prayed, one word began to predominate their thoughts. It was Lesotho and not Mozambique. As they read their Bibles and prayed, the country of Lesotho kept being whispered into their consciousness. They believed that the voice of God was telling them to go to Lesotho, and Dr. Saunders agreed.

When Randy prayed about this new assignment to Lesotho, he felt God was telling him that He had chosen a whole state of prayer partners to join in the task of establishing a mission in Lesotho. God was not only calling two missionaries, Randy and Nancy, He was calling thousands of prayer partners to join them. As Nancy and Randy talked about what God had revealed to them, they began focusing on the practical steps that would be necessary to see a prayer partnership implemented. They determined the first priority was to locate the state that God had prepared for this task. So, they decided a logical first step was to call the intercessory prayer office at the Foreign Mission Board.

Minette Drumwright was the special assistant for intercessory prayer at the Foreign Mission Board. Randy called the Richmond office and talked with Minette. He laid before Minette his vision of a prayer partner state as a mission strategy that God wanted to use. He envisioned a whole state of Baptists praying to start a new mission in the country of Lesotho. Minette

CHAPTER 36

replied that nothing like this had ever been done before in Southern Baptist missions' life. After Randy finished, Minette commented that it was a marvelous idea. Randy let Minette know that he needed her help in locating a state convention. He believed that God had already prepared a state convention for this commitment. But Randy didn't have any idea what state that might be, so he asked Minette for her help. Minette told Randy that as he was telling her about his vision, only one state that she knew might be ready to catch the vision for a venture of this magnitude came to mind. Earlier in the year, Minette had attended Missouri WMU conferences. She had learned of changes that had been implemented in Missouri WMU in 1984. Each associational WMU was reorganized to include a prayer coordinator. Local churches were encouraged to have prayer coordinators. A state WMU prayer coordinator was elected who sent out a monthly missions prayer guide. In other words, God had already established a prayer network in Missouri. Consequently, when Randy asked Minette which state has God prepared to help in establishing this new work, Minette readily answered, "Missouri."

Randy was overcome with emotion because Minette had no prior knowledge of the Sprinkles being connected to Missouri. Both Randy and Nancy were born and grew up in Missouri. Minette had only known them through their furloughs in Texas. Randy now knew for certain that the answer had been directed by God. God picked Missouri! Now, the Sprinkles would be working with families and churches that they had known while growing up.

Randy needed administrative approval from the person responsible for missions work in Lesotho, the area director, Davis Saunders. Randy wanted Davis to catch the vision and become a supporting partner in this venture. Davis approved Randy's proposal and asked that Randy also come to the Foreign Mission Board Meeting in Richmond and share this partnership vision.

Randy called Minette and said he thought this linking of Missouri and Lesotho would be a Foreign Mission Board project and not a personal project of the Sprinkles. Minette agreed and offered to call Missouri. It was decided that the Woman's Missionary Union was the logical first choice to call.

It began in November 1986 with a call from Minette Drumwright to Missouri WMU Executive Director Alberta Gilpin. Her call to Alberta came as a result of her knowledge of and appreciation for the Missouri Missions Prayer Network. This network had been established a few years earlier to facilitate specific and concerted prayer for Baptist missions and missionaries around the world. It was administered by Missouri WMU, but its goal was involvement of all

CHAPTER 36

Missouri Baptists.

The call from Mrs. Drumwright was a thrilling one. Foreign Mission Board executive, Dr. Davis Saunders, had given approval for the establishment of the first-ever state/nation prayer partnership. The question was, "Would Missouri prayerfully consider becoming the state that would enter into this partnership to pray for Lesotho?"

Missouri's positive response to Minette's call set in motion the vast host of intercessors who united under the banner, "Lift Up Lesotho." Their responsibility was to labor in prayer while the missionaries labored in the country. Together with God, a new partnership was born, resulting in a ministry that would bear rich fruit.

The first months of 1987 saw non-stop activity as the logistics of such a large endeavor were addressed. On the first of January, the Foreign Mission Board officially listed Lesotho as the 109th field of Southern Baptist mission work.

In February, Randy Sprinkle was brought to Richmond, Virginia, to brief the full Foreign Mission Board of Trustees on the Prayer Partnership. By March, he, along with Alberta Gilpin, Norma Altis, then state WMU President; and Marilyn Coble, state Prayer Coordinator, toured the state. The group met in regional meetings with associational WMU Directors, Prayer Coordinators, Directors of Missions, and other WMU leaders. Efforts were made at every level to inform Missouri Baptists and to issue them an invitation to become Lesotho intercessors. What was presented to these leaders was a proposal for something that had never been done before in Southern Baptist life: a state convention linking itself with a new mission at its very beginning in an open-ended partnership.

April 1987 saw two significant events in the history of the prayer partnership. The first was the MWMU Annual Meeting held at First Baptist Church of Jefferson City. In response to a formal invitation, hundreds of women committed themselves not only to faithful prayer for Lesotho but also to the task of going back to their churches and organizing others to join in this task. When Randy Sprinkle spoke during the Annual Meeting, he presented a Prayer Covenant for Lesotho that he had written. He read the Covenant and asked women to consider responding to a call to pray for Lesotho. Hundreds of women waited in line for two hours to sign the covenant. Some of the women even chose to skip lunch to make this commitment.

CHAPTER 36

LIFT UP LESOTHO PRAYER COVENANT

"Ask, and it shall be given to you; seek, and you shall find; knock, and it shall be opened to you" (Matthew 7:7 NASB).

By the grace of God and to His glory, we joyfully enter into a covenant of intercessory prayer for God's spiritual blessings in the African nation of Lesotho. In so doing, we give priority in our own lives to prayer and to gathering others together to pray to this end.

As we go to God in prayer, we will seek to come to Him prepared, in heart and mind, to intercede without hindrance according to His desires.

We will be alert to His responses as we pray that our intercessions may always be guided by the progressive unfolding of His will in Lesotho and in our lives.

By His grace, we will persist in prayer until spiritual awakening is brought to reality in Lesotho.

Recognizing that awakening is born in and sustained by a movement of prayer, we will not only intercede personally, but we will also be faithful to call upon God to raise up others to join with us in prayer.

The second significant event occurred the week following the Annual Meeting as the Missouri Baptist Convention Executive Board met. There, in regular session, the state Executive Board formally voted to call on all Missouri Baptists to join the Missouri/ Lesotho Prayer Partnership.

Following this Executive Board meeting, the Sprinkles left for Africa and arrived in Lesotho on May 1, 1987. The first months of their work were difficult because of crime, lack of adequate housing, and difficulties in obtaining their resident permits. More than once it looked as if they would not be able to stay in Lesotho. Time after time, Missouri intercessors went before God on their behalf, and His intervention brought resolution to problems, and the work progressed.

Regular video prayer letters were sent back to Missouri and distributed across the state. These video letters kept the intercessors abreast of developments while allowing them visual images of the country and people where God had called the Sprinkles to minister.

In 1988, Randy and Nancy both developed serious health problems. Randy was having leg pain and could barely walk, and went to see an orthopedic doctor. The doctor suspected that Randy's leg pain was caused by a problem in his back. Randy went for outpatient tests in South Africa. The tests showed the cause of Randy's

CHAPTER 36

physical problems was due to damage to the discs and vertebrae in his lower spine, creating pressure on the nerves than ran into his legs. The doctor sent Randy back to Maseru, Lesotho, and ordered him to bed rest for three weeks to see if the inflammation and lower back pain could be reduced. Later Randy was admitted to the hospital, where it was discovered he had herniated discs in his neck and in his lower back. Randy was sent back to his home with a fitted traction device and orders to stay in bed for the next five weeks. The rest of the family had been sick with strep throat. Nancy's health was also affected by her lupus. She was physically and mentally exhausted. With their many health challenges, they determined that the time had come to leave Lesotho.

The Sprinkles went to a missionary house near Southwestern Baptist Theological Seminary in Fort Worth, Texas. They immediately made medical appointments with the appropriate specialists. Nancy's rheumatologist confirmed a relapse of lupus, and she began treatment. Randy met with a neurosurgeon, and he confirmed that Randy would need neck surgery. A herniated disc would be removed, and the two flanking vertebrae fused. Then a few months later, he would need surgery on his lower back.

When Randy returned to the mission house, he called Marilyn Coble, the Missouri WMU Prayer Coordinator. The Missouri intercessors were following the Sprinkles' health developments closely. Marilyn had been anticipating the call from Randy and already had planned how she would use the telephone prayer chain to spread the news quickly. As Randy told Marilyn the date of his surgery, he heard Marilyn shout in a mixture of astonishment and amazement. Marilyn told Randy, "The dates of your hospitalization and surgery are the same dates as the Missouri WMU Annual Meeting on April 15-16, 1988 at Second Baptist Church in Liberty. God had done it again. God is way out ahead of us. God has already done far better than I ever could have. There will be over a thousand of us gathered and ready to pray for you in Liberty." Randy could see God moving behind the scenes, and he felt at peace.

The next week Randy entered the hospital and was given two injections in preparation for a myelogram, a basic test that would provide the surgeon with information he needed to perform the surgery. It would also be compared with a myelogram he had previously in Africa. Randy was kept in the x-ray room for an extended period of time. Finally, the surgeon came into the room and told him, "We had been planning on removing a herniated disc that was causing your problems. But now, it is a perfectly normal disc. This is very difficult to explain. In contrast to your previous x-rays and MRI, the myelogram today looks normal and healthy." Randy

CHAPTER 36

was released from the hospital and sent home. Clearly God had intervened and healed the damaged disc in Randy's neck.

The morning after Randy returned home, he answered the phone. It was Marilyn Coble calling Nancy to see how Randy's surgery had gone. She wanted to know how come Randy was home answering the phone. Randy detailed for Marilyn what had transpired at the hospital. Marilyn then returned to the WMU Annual Meeting and related how God had answered their prayers for Randy. Randy began physical therapy, which lessened the inflammation in his spine and strengthened his back. Nevertheless, the Foreign Mission Board encouraged the Sprinkles to plan for stateside employment.

Prior to their leaving, another missionary couple was called out, Stacy and Shelia. However, they also experienced medical problems with their son and had to resign and were unable to go back to Lesotho.

Those were dark days for the Lesotho mission and for Missouri intercessors. As Missouri WMU women came to the 1989 Annual Meeting in Poplar Bluff, it was with a sense that despite their obedience to God's call to Lesotho, the Mission seemed destined for failure. With this backdrop and in the midst of questions about the future of the prayer partnership, God powerfully met the women at the 1989 Annual Meeting. In an emotional closing service, they realized that despite the costs and the missionary hardships, their commission as laborers, intercessors, for Lesotho remained unchanged. Despite appearances, they were to press on and to pray on. Randy Sprinkle gave the closing message; he once again had the leather-bound journal with the Lesotho Prayer Covenant in it which held hundreds of signatures of intercessors. In closing, Randy gave a call to arms. He asked women to come and answer the call and sign and seal their commitment to pray for Lesotho. As the hymn "Onward, Christian Soldiers" was sung, every aisle of the church was filled with long lines of intercessors waiting to sign their commitment.

The results since have been glorious. Rather than allowing the closing of the Mission, God instead called Wayne and Alice M. out of Kenya and Ron and Gloria M. out of Rwanda and sent them to Lesotho. Together these missionaries have advanced the outreach and influence of the Mission. Today there are Baptist congregations in numerous towns and villages. Ron, a medical doctor, conducted medical clinics in remote areas and spread the gospel.

At the 1992 Annual Meeting in Jefferson City, Wayne and Alice McMillian shared about God's work in Lesotho. Missouri WMU presented them a gift of a Lord's Supper service to use with the congregations in Lesotho. The McMillian family took a leave of absence for about two years due to schooling needs of their

CHAPTER 36

children. Once again, Missouri Baptists were challenged to pray. The last days of 1993 brought Charles and Glenda M., 25-year veterans of FMB mission work, to transfer to Lesotho to work in church development. God called newly appointed missionaries Cliff and Mary Sue J. to serve in Lesotho. Delos and Wanda B. invested themselves in ministering and witnessing to the Basotho people.

In January 1999, Gene and Jean P., who had served in Rhodesia and Zimbabwe for forty years, went to Lesotho. After nine years of service in Lesotho with Campus Crusade for Christ, the Wes and Beth G. family joined the work of the International Mission Board in May 2000 and arrived in Lesotho in August 2000. They served as the Team Leaders/Strategists for the Basotho Team.

David and Carla B. joined the Basotho Team on July 1, 2003. They previously served with the IMB in Malawi and in the Johannesburg area of South Africa. Alan and Babs D. arrived in Lesotho on May 12, 2004. They led the Maluti Mountain Team of the Basotho Team. Early January of 2007, Tom and Cindi M. arrived to serve as the Lesotho Lowlands sub-team leader. Their work included planting new churches in the Lowlands of Lesotho as well as helping to disciple and train pastors and members of existing Baptist churches. Tom served as the Basotho Team Strategy Leader. Larry and Sally P. arrived in Lesotho, March

7, 2009 and were re-assigned to Tanzania in January 2011.

Jim, Teresa, Gracie, Anna, and Rebekah F. arrived in Lesotho, March 28, 2009. Their assignment was the Maluti Mountains. Jonathan and Liz B. were appointed as apprentice missionaries and went to Lesotho in the summer of 2013. They were assigned to the Katse area and relocated to the Mokhotlong region. Stan and Angie B. came to Lesotho and served alongside the Floras. Jake and Ginger G. are working in four villages in Lesotho.

Throughout the last 35 years, Missouri WMU has been holding the ropes for the Lesotho missionaries. Gene Phillips, missionary to Lesotho, spoke at the WMU Annual Meeting on April 28, 2000, he said, "We feel that we missionaries and WMU members are a team." He asked Missouri WMU to keep up the wonderful work God has called them to do.

Epilogue

My prayer for the future of Missouri Woman's Missionary Union would be Proverbs 3:6, "In all your ways acknowledge Him and He will direct your paths." (MEV)

This missions journey has been a story of past dedicated women who have seen the value of missions education and have continued to make it a reality. This is a story of Missouri women who have dedicated themselves to the cause of missions discipleship. Women who have promoted the missions offerings through the years to enable missionaries to continue to spread the gospel at home and overseas.

Women who have prayed for thousands and thousands of missionaries on their birthdays through the past one hundred years. Women who have rejoiced when they heard about some of the results of those prayers at our Missouri Mission Celebration meetings. During the last one hundred years, there have been about 1,200 Missourians called to be Foreign/International Missionaries to the unreached people of the world.

Women who have done numerous mission projects ministering to the homeless, those in Pregnancy Care Centers, nursing homes, prisons, making disaster relief hygiene kits, and sending thousands of Operation Christmas Child boxes all around the world. The many countless ministry projects of the Missouri Woman's Missionary Union have made a difference in other people's lives. Missouri WMU has found strength for the present by looking at the strength of women from our past. Thank You, Missouri WMU members, for keeping missions alive in our state.

If you have questions about how to start a missions discipleship group in your church, you can contact the Missouri WMU Facebook page. You can also find information on how to start a new WMU organization and contact information for the WMU staff at https://mobaptist.org/wmu/.

Jan Turner

APPENDICES

Appendix I

MISSOURI WMU ANNUAL MEETING LOCATIONS

1. October 15, 1923 - First Baptist Church, Poplar Bluff
2. November 29, 1924 - Park Baptist Church, Brookfield
3. November 19, 1925 - First Baptist Church, Carthage
4. October 18-19, 1926 - Third Baptist Church, St. Louis
5. October 17-18, 1927- First Baptist Church, Kansas City
6. October 22-23, 1928 - First Baptist Church, Cape Girardeau
7. October 21-22, 1929 - Presser Hall, Hardin College, Mexico
8. June 24-26, 1930 - First Baptist Church, Marshall
9. April 7-9, 1931 - Calvary Baptist Church, Kansas City
10. April 3-5, 1932 - First Baptist Church, St. Louis
11. April 5-7, 1933 - First Baptist Church, Springfield
12. April 4-6,1934 - Fifth Street Baptist Church, Hannibal
13. April 3-5, 1935 - First Baptist Church, Cape Girardeau
14. April 1-3, 1936 - First Baptist Church, Chillicothe
15. April 7-9, 1937 - First Baptist Church, Sedalia
16. April 6-8, 1938 - First Baptist Church, Mexico
17. April 5-7, 1939 - First Baptist Church, Joplin
18. April 3-5, 1940 - First Baptist Church, St. Joseph
19. April 2-4, 1941 - Second Baptist Church, St. Louis
20. April 1-3, 1942 - First Baptist Church, Springfield
21. April 7-9, 1943 - First Baptist Church, Moberly
22. April 5-7, 1944 - First Baptist Church, Jefferson City
23. 1945 - - Cancelled because of World War II
24. April 4-6, 1946 - First Baptist Church, Joplin
25. April 9-11,1947 - Music Hall, Municipal Auditorium, Kansas City
26. April 7-9, 1948 - Third Baptist Church, St. Louis
27. April 6-8, 1949 - First Baptist Church, St. Joseph

Appendix I

28. March 29-31, 1950 - First Baptist Church, Cape Girardeau
29. April 4-6, 1951 - Music Hall, Municipal Auditorium, Kansas City
30. April 2-4, 1952 - First Baptist Church, Springfield
31. April 8-10, 1953 - Third Baptist Church, St. Louis
32. April 7-9, 1954 - First Baptist Church, St. Joseph
33. March 30-April 1, 1955 - First Baptist Church, Moberly
34. April 4-6, 1956 - Memorial Hall, Carthage
35. April 3-5, 1957 - Third Baptist Church, St. Louis
36. April 9-11, 1958 - First Baptist Church, Sedalia
37. April 2-4, 1959 - World War II Memorial Building, Kansas City
38. April 7-9, 1960 - First Baptist Church, Cape Girardeau
39. April 6-8, 1961 - First Baptist Church, Columbia
40. March 29-31, 1962 - First Baptist Church, Springfield
41. March21-23, 1963 - First Baptist Church, St. Johns
42. March 19-21, 1964 - First Baptist Church, St. Joseph
43. April 1-3, 1965 - First Baptist Church, Joplin
44. March 31- April 2, 1966 - Maywood Baptist Church, Independence
45. March 30-April 1, 1967 - First Baptist Church, Mexico
46. March 28-30, 1968 - First Baptist Church, Cape Girardeau
47. April 24-25, 1969 - First Baptist Church, Springfield
48. April 2-4, 1970 - Third Baptist Church, St. Louis
49. April 1-3, 1971 - First Baptist Church, Columbia
50. April 6-8, 1972 - First Baptist Church, St. Joseph
51. April 5-7, 1973 - First Baptist Church, Poplar Bluff
52. March 28-30, 1974 - Windermere Baptist Assembly, Roach
53. April 17-19, 1975 - First Baptist Church, Springfield
54. April 1-3, 1976 - First Baptist Church, Raytown
55. April 14-16, 1977 - First Baptist Church, St. Johns
56. **April 6-8, 1978 - Calvary Baptist Church, Columbia**
57. April 9-11, 1979 - First Baptist Church, Blue Springs
58. April 15- April 10-12, 1980 - First Baptist Church, Cape Girardeau
59. April 2-4, 1981 - First Baptist Church, Joplin

Missouri WMU Annual Meeting Locations

60. April 15-17, 1982 - First Baptist Church, Ferguson
61. April 15-16, 1983 - First Baptist Church, Sedalia
62. April 13-14, 1984 - Wyatt Park Baptist Church, St. Joseph
63. April 19-20, 1985 - Calvary Baptist Church, Columbia
64. April 4-5, 1986 - First Baptist Church, Springfield
65. April 10-11, 1987 - First Baptist Church, Jefferson City
66. April 15-16, 1988 - Second Baptist Church, Liberty
67. April 14-15, 1989 - First Baptist Church, Poplar Bluff
68. April 20-21, 1990 - Forest Park Baptist Church, Joplin
69. April 19-20, 1991 - First Baptist Church, Harvester
70. April 10-11, 1992 - First Baptist Church, Jefferson City
71. April 16-17, 1993 - First Baptist Church, Raytown
72. April 15-16, 1994 - Hannibal LaGrange College, Hannibal
73. April 29, 1995 - First Baptist Church, Jefferson City
74. April 19-20, 1996 - First Baptist Church, Cape Girardeau
75. April 18-19, 1997 - First Baptist Church, Springfield
76. April 17-18, 1998 - First Baptist Church, Raytown
77. April 17, 1999 - First Baptist Church, Jefferson City
78. April 28-29, 2000 - Fee Fee Baptist Church, Bridgeton
79. April 20-21, 2001 - South Haven Baptist Church, Springfield
80. April 12-13, 2002 - Memorial Baptist Church, Columbia
81. April 25-26, 2003 - William Jewell College, Liberty
82. April 23-24, 2004 - First Baptist Church, Poplar Bluff
83. April 15-16, 2005 - First Baptist Church, Ellisville
84. April 28-29, 2006 - Forest Park Baptist Church, Joplin
85. April 27-28, 2007 - Hannibal-LaGrange College, Hannibal
86. April 18-19, 2008 - First Baptist Church, Raytown
87. April 17-18, 2009 - First Baptist Church, Lebanon
88. April 9-10, 2010 - Frederick Boulevard Baptist Church, St. Joseph
89. April 15-16, 2011 - First Baptist Church, Springfield
90. April 20-21, 2012 - First Baptist Church, Jackson
91. April 12-13, 2013 - First Baptist Church, Warrensburg

Appendix I

92. April 4-5, 2014 - Second Baptist Church, Springfield
93. April 10-11, 2015 - First Baptist Church, St. Charles
94. April 8-9, 2016 - Midwestern Baptist Theological Seminary, Kansas City
95. April 7-8, 2017 - First Baptist Church, Lebanon
96. April 6-7, 2018 - South Gate Baptist Church, Springfield
97. April 5-6, 2019 - First Baptist Church, Kearney
98. April 2020 - Cancelled because of Covid Pandemic
99. September 10-11, 2021 - First Baptist Church, Lake St. Louis
100. April 1-2, 2022 - Concord Baptist Church, Jefferson City
101. April 14-15, 2023 - First Baptist Church, Poplar Bluff

Appendix II

MISSOURI WMU PRESIDENTS 1923-2023

1923-1934   Laura Dell Malotte Armstrong, Plattsburg

1935-1941   Cora Francis Cowgill McWilliams, Liberty

1941-1946   Louise Enloe McKee, New Bloomfield

1946   Josephine Riley Medlin, Jefferson City

1946-1952   LeeAnna Floy Kinell, Joplin

1952-1956   Lena Shaner Burnham, St. Joseph, Willard

1956-1960   Elizabeth Tillery Crozier, West Plains

1960-1964   Eunice Powell Allison, Springfield

1964-1969   Ferroll Woodford DeLozier, St. Louis

1969-1974   Viola Volkart Scherff, Clarksburg

1974-1976   Marilyn Harris Coble, Chesterfield

1976-1981   Lorene Hamblen Murphy, Kansas City

Appendix II

1981-1986	Barbara Birt Bray, Knob Noster
1986-1991	Norma Hays Altis, Liberty
1991-1996	Dawn O'Neill Phillips, St. Joseph, Chillicothe
1996-1999	Barbara Daniels Popp, Jackson
1999-2004	Debbie Bailey Miller, Jefferson City
2004-2009	Lorraine Rogers Powers, Blue Springs
2009-2014	Joan Harms Dotson, Lake St. Louis
2014-2019	Cherri Hall Crump, Rolla
2019	Mary Ann Collier Randall, Lebanon
2019-2020	Connie Meeker Craig, Hannibal
2020-present	Jan Currence Turner, Nixa

Appendix III

MISSOURI WMU EXECUTIVE DIRECTORS 1923-2023

1923-1936	Mable Reynolds, Corresponding Secretary
1937-1947	Madge N. Truex
1947-1954	Eva Berry
1954	Louise McKee, Interim Executive Secretary
1954-1958	Hilda Beggs
1959-1973	Mary O. Bidstrup
1973-2000	Alberta J. Gilpin
2000-2003	Kathy Scott
2003-2010	Vivian McCaughan
2010-2019	Laura Wells
2019-2021	Bonnie Carter
8/21-12/2021	Cheryl Stahlman, Interim Executive Director
2022-Present	Cheryl Stahlman

Appendix IV

MISSOURI EMERITUS MISSIONARIES 2006-2023

2006   Nona Renfrow, Brazil, 1955-1986

2007   Mariam Misner, Indonesia, 1956-1993

2008   Beulah Peoples, 40 years in denominational work

2009   Lucy Wagner, South Korea, 1955-1994

2010   Leona Troop Macklin, Brazil, 1959-1994

2011   Beverly Richardson, Jordan, 1975-2002

2012   Ron and Ina Winstead, East Asia, 1972-2001

2013   Carolyn Houts, Ghana, 1976-2011

2014   Veda Locke, Nigeria, 1955-1991

2015   Emmett and LaNell Barnes, Lebanon, Morocco, 1966-1999

2016   Joe and Carol Barbour, Zambia, 1988-1998

2017   Carl and Martha Rees, Middle America, Honduras, Mexico, 1978-2006

2018   Harold Cummins, Bangladesh, Kenya, 1959-1991

2019   Mariam Misner, Indonesia, 1956-1993

2020   Bill and Carol Bowers, Romania, South Africa, 1997-2012

2021   David and Janene Ford, Argentina, Venezuela, 1978-1991, 1995-2009

2022   Phil and Oretha Brewster, Philippines, 1976-2006

2023   Randy and Nancy Sprinkle, Ethiopia, Botswana, Lesotho, 1975-1988

Appendix V

MISSOURI WMU NOTEWORTHY EVENTS 1923-2023

1923 Woman's Missionary Union of Missouri organized in October 15 at First Baptist Church of Poplar Bluff. Laura Dell Armstrong of Plattsburg was elected President.

1924 First city-wide School of Missions was held in St. Louis.

1925 Missouri WMU was instrumental in planning the first Baptist Student Union Convention in Mexico.

1926 WMU sponsored a tithing story contest.

1927 In order to encourage the beginning of Brotherhood in Missouri, awards were presented to laymen who completed mission study requirements.

1928 First YWA House Party held in Springfield.

1929 The last Annual Meeting MWMU held in conjunction with the Missouri Baptist General Convention.

1930 The first separate WMU Annual Meeting was held at First Baptist Church of Marshall on June 24-26.

1931 1,000 conversions reported as a result of witnessing efforts of WMU women in Missouri.

1932 First state RA and GA camps held at Baptist Hill Assembly in Mount Vernon.

Appendix V

1933   Laura Armstrong was elected President of national WMU. The first Queens with Scepter were Lucille Mott and Lena Mae Hicks from Mountain Grove Baptist Church.

1934   First Queen Regent was Lena Mae Hicks from Mountain Grove Baptist Church.

1935   1,294 WMU organizations with a membership of 13,276 were reported.

1936   1,362 WMU organizations were reported.

1937   First Business Women's Circle formed in Springfield.

1938   There were 773 churches with WMU organizations.

1939   There were 2,358 WMU organizations in Missouri.

1940   There were 2,455 WMU organizations in Missouri.

1941   There were 2,515 WMU organizations in Missouri.

1942   First cooperative African-American Institute and first handbook for African-Americans was published.

1943   There were 212 new WMU organizations formed.

1944   There were 283 new WMU organizations formed.

1945   WMU Annual Meeting was cancelled because of World War II.

1946   First WMU conference at Hollister Baptist Assembly.

1947   Loan scholarship established for nurses planning to enter missions.

Missouri WMU Noteworthy Events 1923-2023

1948   Missouri Business Woman's Circle Federation organized.

1949   Missouri Baptist Convention headquarters and WMU office moved from Kansas City to Jefferson City.

1950   Missouri Baptist Woman's Missionary Council for white and African-American women was created.

1951   Mrs. McWilliams' book about history of Missouri Baptist woman's missions work, *Women in Missions in Missouri,* was published.

1952   WMU Special Funds created to cover Training School and Nurses scholarships, Margaret Fund and other special offerings.

1953   WMU Special Funds becomes the Madge N. Truex Fund in honor of the former WMU Executive Secretary from 1937-1947.

1954   Joint committee of WMU and Brotherhood formed to handle RA work.

1955   WMU becomes a department of Missouri Baptist General Association.

1956   Mary Walsh completed the missionary biography collection, *Assignment: Light Bearers.* It was a useful mission's support tool generated through Missouri WMU.

1957   African-American Baptist Women were invited to attend the WMU conference at Hollister.

1958   Missouri Baptist General Association changed its name to Missouri Baptist Convention.

Appendix V

1959   First Missouri sponsored bus trip to WMU Week at
        Ridgecrest Baptist Conference Center in North
        Carolina. Business Woman's Federation merged
        with Missouri WMU and became the Association of
        Night Circles of Missouri.

1960   WMU helped build the Children's Building at Windermere.

1961   Advanced Leadership Training program begun.

1962   GAs celebrated 50th Anniversary of their organization.

1963   Literacy work was begun in Missouri.

1964   There were 4,910 WMU organizations with a total
        membership of 70,882.

1965   First Area Clinics were held at 24 different
        locations and provided in-depth WMU training.

1966   There were 4,862 WMU organizations with a total
        membership of 67,589.

1967   Alberta Gilpin became YWA/Sunbeam Director.

1968   *Missouri WMU Handbook* becomes *Missouri WMU
        Facts and Features.*

1969   Missouri WMU had a membership of 71,124.

1970   WMU age level organizations were revamped and
        renamed.

1971   Missouri Baptist Convention headquarters moved to
        The Baptist Building, 400 East High Street,
        Jefferson City.

1972	Missions conferences held for single and married young adults.
1973	Fiftieth anniversary celebration of Missouri WMU held at First Baptist Church, Poplar Bluff.
1974	First GA Caravans were held.
1975	WMU Executive Secretary name was changed to WMU Director to make department heads equal in status and pay.
1976	*Facts and Features* renamed *Resource Book.* *Associational Plan Book* was created.
1977	Six Regional Leadership Training Conferences replaced the 24 Area Clinics held in the past.
1978	Missouri WMU was the SBC leader in the number of WMU leadership diplomas earned through the Church Study Course program.
1979	Teen Scene split into Junior High and Senior High meetings.
1980	Starteam begun to help initiate new WMU organizations.
1981	There was a total attendance of 1,138 at the WMU Annual Meeting held at First Baptist Church, Joplin.
1982	Missouri WMU took part in a Prayer Task Force pilot program.
1983	First state prayer coordinator was elected and added to the list of officers on the WMU Board.

Appendix V

1984   Camp Windermere for girls celebrated its twenty-fifth anniversary.

1985   First statewide GA Retreat held at Windermere.

1986   Ethnic/Language and African-American Southern Baptist contract workers employed.

1987   Missouri WMU began Prayer Partnership with Randy and Nancy Sprinkle, missionaries to Lesotho, Africa.

1988   Missouri took five buses of women to Richmond, Virginia, for the national WMU Centennial Celebration.

1989   Five buses of Missouri Acteens attended national Acteens Convention in San Antonio, Texas.

1990   Over 2,550 Girls in Action and leaders attended three GA Retreats and a Mother/Daughter weekend.

1991   Mary O. Bidstrup Scholarship was initiated to provide money for materials for churches who were beginning a new WMU program in their church.

1992   There were 1,147 in attendance at the WMU Annual Meeting held April 1-2 at First Baptist Church, Jefferson City.

1993   Missouri began a five-year partnership with the country of Belarus and the state of Wyoming.

1994   Almost 1,700 GAs and leaders attended GA Retreats over four weekends.

1995   2,128 GAs and leaders attended three GA Retreats.

Missouri WMU Noteworthy Events 1923-2023

1996   Missouri WMU adopted a prayer project for the evangelization of people in Tianjin, China.

1997   Attendance at the Missouri WMU Annual Meeting was 1,004 held at First Baptist Church, Springfield.

1998   Workshops were added to the Mission Celebrations/Annual Meeting to enable participants to hear more in-depth reports from missionaries and receive age level training.

1999   Missouri WMU had an enrollment of 28,360 members.

2000   Alberta Gilpin retired after 33 years of service with Missouri WMU. WMU filed to become a 501C(3) nonprofit corporation.

2001   The Alberta Gilpin Fund was established.

2002   Over 1,100 boys and leaders attended RA Congress where more than 150 decisions were made.

2003   Vivian McCaughan had the added job responsibility of WMU/Women's Ministry Specialist.

2004   The MWMU Disaster Recovery Manual assembled.

2005   Five GA Retreats were held with over 1,077 girls and leaders in attendance.

2006   Nona Renfrow, missionary to Brazil from 1955-1986, was the first Missionary Emeritus to be recognized.

2007   *Enduring Love, the Alberta Gilpin Story* was published and made available for purchase at the

Appendix V

Missions Celebration. Alberta was present to autograph copies of her biography.

2008 Beulah Peoples was recognized as Missionary Emeritus. She spent forty years doing denominational work.

2009 GA Retreats were held in eight locations over three weekends with approximately 1,300 girls and leaders in attendance.

2010 According to the Missouri Baptist Convention Book of Reports, there were 19,248 members enrolled in WMU organizations.

2011 Twenty-six new MWMU organizations were begun.

2012 RAs and Challengers were added under the WMU organization.

2013 Missouri WMU had twenty-three new MWMU organizations.

2014 Thirty-one new MWMU organizations started.

2015 Missouri women and churches help pack and provide supplies for 804 buckets for the Baptist Global Response project called Buckets of Love.

2016 More than 400 boys and leaders attended the 2016 RA Congress in Sedalia. Five hundred girls and leaders attended the GA Retreats.

2017 Twenty-eight new MWMU groups were organized.

2018 Eight regional training events were offered across Missouri with over 350 in attendance.

2019   Mariam Lou Misner served for thirty-seven years as a Medical Lab Technician and teacher in Indonesia from 1956-1993 and was recognized as Missionary Emeritus for 2019.

2020   All the WMU state events were cancelled because of the Covid 19 pandemic which resulted in a stay-at-home order issued by the government.

2021   Twelve new MWMU groups were organized in 2021.

2022   Developed a partnership relationship with Montana Southern Baptist Women

2023   *Missouri Woman's Missionary Union's Centennial Journey 1923-2023* was compiled and written by MWMU President Jan Turner for the 100th Anniversary Meeting at First Baptist Church in Poplar Bluff, April 14-15, 2023.

Chapter Notes

Chapter 1

[1] Catherine B. Allen, *A Century to Celebrate* (Birmingham, Alabama: Woman's Missionary Union, 1987), page 117.

[2] Ibid., page 117.

Laura Mason, *Ye Are the Branches: A History of Missouri Baptist Woman's Missionary Organizations* (Missouri Baptist Press, 1987), pages 3-35.

Chapter 2

Laura Mason, *Ye Are the Branches: A History of Missouri Baptist Woman's Missionary Organizations* (Missouri Baptist Press, 1987), pages 32-33.

Chapter 3

[1] Laura Mason, *Ye Are the Branches: A History of Missouri Baptist Woman's Missionary Organizations* (Missouri Baptist Press, 1987), pages 35-36.

[2] Catherine B. Allen, *Laborers Together With God* (Woman's Missionary Union, Auxiliary to Southern Baptist Convention, 1987), p. 78.

[3] Ibid., pages 79-80.

[4] Ibid., page 80.

[5] Ibid., pages 80-81.

[6] Ibid., page 80.

[7] Laura Mason, *Ye Are the Branches: A History of Missouri Baptist Woman's Missionary Organizations* (Missouri Baptist Press, 1987), pages 35-36.

[8] Ibid., pages 35-41.

Chapter 4

Information compiled from Laura Mason, *Ye Are the Branches: A History of Missouri Baptist Woman's Missionary Organizations* (Missouri Baptist Press, 1987), pages 42-46.

Chapter 5

Information compiled from Laura Mason, *Ye Are the Branches: A History of Missouri Baptist Woman's Missionary Organizations* (Missouri Baptist Press, 1987), pages 45-47, 52.

Chapter 6

Information compiled from Laura Mason, *Ye Are the Branches: A History of Missouri Baptist Woman's Missionary Organizations* (Missouri Baptist Press, 1987), pages 47-49.

Mrs. George McWilliams, *Women and Missions in Missouri*, (Woman's Missionary Union, Missouri Baptist General Association, 1951), page 222.

Chapter 7

Information compiled from Laura Mason, *Ye Are the Branches: A History of Missouri Baptist Woman's Missionary Organizations* (Missouri Baptist Press, 1987), pages 50-51.

Chapter 8

Information compiled from Laura Mason, *Ye Are the Branches: A History of Missouri Baptist Woman's Missionary Organizations* (Missouri Baptist Press, 1987), pages 50-51.

Chapter 9

Information compiled from Laura Mason, *Ye Are the Branches: A History of Missouri Baptist Woman's Missionary Organizations* (Missouri Baptist Press, 1987), pages 55-59.

Chapter 10

Information compiled from Laura Mason, *Ye Are the Branches: A History of Missouri Baptist Woman's Missionary Organizations* (Missouri Baptist Press, 1987), pages 60-63.

Chapter 11

Information compiled from Laura Mason, *Ye Are the Branches: A History of Missouri Baptist Woman's Missionary Organizations* (Missouri Baptist Press, 1987), pages 62-70.

Chapter 12

Information compiled from Laura Mason, *Ye Are the Branches: A History of Missouri Baptist Woman's Missionary Organizations* (Missouri Baptist Press, 1987), pages 70-73,75.

Chapter 13

Information compiled from Laura Mason, *Ye Are the Branches: A History of Missouri Baptist Woman's Missionary Organizations* (Missouri Baptist Press, 1987), pages 75-77.

Chapter 14

Information compiled from Laura Mason, *Ye Are the Branches: A History of Missouri Baptist Woman's Missionary Organizations* (Missouri Baptist Press, 1987), pages 78-82.

Chapter Notes

Chapter 15

Information compiled from Laura Mason, *Ye Are the Branches: A History of Missouri Baptist Woman's Missionary Organizations* (Missouri Baptist Press, 1987), pages 82-87.

Chapter 16

Information compiled from Laura Mason, *Ye Are the Branches: A History of Missouri Baptist Woman's Missionary Organizations* (Missouri Baptist Press, 1987), pages 87-90.

Chapter 17

Information compiled from Laura Mason, *Ye Are the Branches: A History of Missouri Baptist Woman's Missionary Organizations* (Missouri Baptist Press, 1987), pages 93-95.

Information compiled from Barbara Bray, *Enduring Love, The Alberta Gilpin Story*. Missouri Woman's Missionary Union, 2007, pages 24-54.

Chapter 18

Information compiled from Laura Mason, *Ye Are the Branches: A History of Missouri Baptist Woman's Missionary Organizations* (Missouri Baptist Press, 1987), pages 94-96.

Chapter 19

Information compiled from Laura Mason, *Ye Are the Branches: A History of Missouri Baptist Woman's Missionary Organizations* (Missouri Baptist Press, 1987), pages 96-101.

Chapter 20

Information compiled from Laura Mason, *Ye Are the Branches: A History of Missouri Baptist Woman's Missionary Organizations* (Missouri Baptist Press, 1987), pages 101-106.

Chapter 21

[1] Laura Mason, *Ye Are the Branches: A History of Missouri Baptist Woman's Missionary Organizations* (Missouri Baptist Press, 1987), page 106.

Information compiled from Laura Mason, *Ye Are the Branches: A History of Missouri Baptist Woman's Missionary Organizations* (Missouri Baptist Press, 1987), pages 106-107.

Information compiled from Laura Mason, *Abide In Me, A Continuation of Ye Are the Branches 1987-1998.* Missouri Woman's Missionary Union, 1998, pages 7-13.

Chapter 22

Information compiled from Laura Mason, *Abide In Me, A Continuation of Ye Are the Branches 1987-1998.* Missouri Woman's Missionary Union, 1998, pages 15-23.

Chapter 23

Information compiled from Laura Mason, *Abide In Me, A Continuation of Ye Are the Branches 1987-1998.* Missouri Woman's Missionary Union, 1998, pages 25-30.

Information compiled from Barbara Bray, *From Change to Challenge A Continuation of the History of the Missouri Woman's Missionary Union from 1998-2007.* Missouri Woman's Missionary Union, 2007, pages 26-27.

Chapter 24

Information compiled from Annual Meeting minutes, President reports and Resource Books from 1999-2004, and from Debbie Miller.

Information compiled from Barbara Bray, *From Change to Challenge A Continuation of the History of the Missouri Woman's Missionary Union from 1998-2007.* Missouri Woman's Missionary Union, 2007, pages 26-31.

Chapter 25

Information compiled from 2003 Annual Meeting minutes and biographical information written by Kathy Scott.

Chapter 26

Information compiled from Jim McCaughan and Theresa Hargrove Blanchard, (Vivian's sister.)

Vivian McCaughan Emeritus Missionary Biography.

Missions Mosaic, March 2010, page 15.

The Pathway, April 27, 2010.

Chapter 27

Information compiled from Barbara Bray, *From Change to Challenge A Continuation of the History of the Missouri Woman's Missionary Union from 1998-2007.* Missouri Woman's Missionary Union, 2007, pages 32-36.

WMU report from 2005 *MBC Book of Reports*, page 252.

Information compiled from WMU report from 2006 *MBC Book of Reports*, page 257-258.

President's report from 2006 WMU Annual Meeting program, page 12.

WMU report from 2007 *MBC Book of Reports*, page 274.

Chapter Notes

President's report from 2008 WMU Annual Meeting program, page 14.

Secretary minutes from 2009 MWMU Annual Meeting.

Biography written by Lorraine Powers.

Chapter 28

Information compiled from the MWMU Resource Directory, 2013, pages 19-20.

Minutes from WMU Annual Meetings 2009-2014.

President's reports from 2010-2014.

WMU Report from 2010 *MBC Book of Reports*, page 70.

WMU Report from 2011 *MBC Book of Reports*, page 74.

WMU Report from 2012 *MBC Book of Reports*, page 78.

WMU Report from 2013 *MBC Book of Reports*, page 78.

Biography written by Joan Dotson.

Chapter 29

Biography written by Laura Wells.

Chapter 30

Information compiled from MWMU Mission Celebration /Annual Meeting minutes from 2014-2019.

President's Reports from 2015-2019 printed in Missions Celebration programs.

Biography written by Cherri Crump.

Chapter 31

Biography written by Bonnie Carter.

Chapter 32

Biography written by Mary Ann Randall.

Chapter 33

Biography written by Connie Craig.

Chapter Notes

Chapter 34

Biography written by Jan Turner.

MWMU Mission Celebration/Annual Meeting minutes from 2021-2022.

President's Reports from 2021-2022 printed in Missions Celebration programs.

2021-2022 MWMU Board meeting minutes.

Chapter 35

Biography written by Cheryl Stahlman.

Chapter 36

WMU Resource Directory, 1999-2000, page 18.

WMU Resource Directory, 2007, pages 35-36.

WMU Resource Directory, 2013, pages 19-20.

Randy Sprinkle, *Until the Stars Appear,* (Birmingham, Alabama, New Hope, 1994) Used by permission from publisher and author to summarize information in this chapter.

Bibliography

Allen, Catherine B. *Laborers Together With God.* Birmingham, Alabama: Woman's Missionary Union, 1987, pages 77-81.

Allen, Catherine B. *A Century to Celebrate.* Birmingham, Alabama: Woman's Missionary Union, 1987, pages 116-117.

Bray, Barbara. *Enduring Love, The Alberta Gilpin Story.* Missouri Woman's Missionary Union, 2007.

Bray, Barbara. *From Change to Challenge, A Continuation of the History of the Missouri Woman's Missionary Union from 1998-2007.* Missouri Woman's Missionary Union, *2007.*

Mason, Laura. *Abide In Me, A Continuation of Ye Are the Branches 1987-1998.* Missouri Woman's Missionary Union, 1998.

Mason, Laura. *Ye Are the Branches, A History of Missouri Baptist Woman's Missionary Organizations.* Missouri Woman's Missionary Union, 1987.

McWilliams, Cora. *Women and Missions in Missouri.* Woman's Missionary Union, Missouri Baptist General Association, 1951, page 222.

Sprinkle, Randy. *Until the Stars Appear.* Birmingham, Alabama: New Hope, 1994.

About The Author

Jan Turner's interest in missions is a result of Missouri WMU. As a young preschooler, she attended Sunbeams, and Girls in Action in grades one through six. She attended GA camps at Lake of the Ozarks. Jan heard many missionary speakers growing up.

Her mission journey continued through her four years of college at Southwest Baptist in Bolivar where she was active in the Baptist Young Women's organization. After serving as a summer missionary near Chicago, Illinois, with the Home Mission Board, Jan felt called to full-time Christian Service. The call to Christian ministry led her to be Baptist Young Women's Director for the Missouri Baptist Convention. A different call to her life came in 1977 as she became a pastor's wife and served in many volunteer WMU positions which are explained in chapter 34 of this book.

Jan earned her bachelor's degree from Southwest Baptist College in Bolivar, Missouri, and her master's degree in Speech Communication from the University of Missouri at Columbia.

Jan, and her husband Phil, have two adult daughters, Joanna and Sarah. Jan and Phil are retired and reside in Nixa, Missouri. They are active members of Hopedale Baptist Church in Ozark.

Made in the USA
Columbia, SC
19 March 2023